Jonathan Bayley

Great Truths on Great Subjects

Jonathan Bayley

Great Truths on Great Subjects

ISBN/EAN: 9783741118272

Manufactured in Europe, USA, Canada, Australia, Japa

Cover: Foto ©Andreas Hilbeck / pixelio.de

Manufactured and distributed by brebook publishing software (www.brebook.com)

Jonathan Bayley

Great Truths on Great Subjects

GREAT TRUTHS ON GREAT SUBJECTS

Six Lectures

DELIVERED AT BRIGHTON

BY THE

REV. DR. BAYLEY

PALACE GARDENS CHURCH, THE MALL, KENSINGTON

Forty-Eighth Thousand.

LONDON:
Published for the Missionary and Tract Society of the New Church
BY JAMES SPEIRS, 36 BLOOMSBURY STREET
1893

LECTURE I.

How to think of the Divine Unity and Trinity 4

LECTURE II.

The Atonement, or Reconciliation 37

LECTURE III.

On the Christian Life 72

LECTURE IV.

Death and Resurrection 108

LECTURE V.

Judgment, Individual and General 145

LECTURE VI.

The Second Coming of the Lord 182

PRELIMINARY ADDRESS AND PRAYER.

MY BELOVED FRIENDS,

The subject to which your attention is invited this evening is one of the very highest importance—one that demands not only the best exertions of the mind, but also the best affections of the heart, in order rightly to understand, to appreciate, and to love the Divine guidance. Our Saviour has promised spiritual animation and Divine light, when He said: "Blessed are the pure in heart, for they shall see God." While, therefore, we endeavour to awaken every attention the mind can give to it, we trust that you will endeavour also to open your hearts to the deepest reception of the influence of the Heavenly King; and to that end, let us all together for a moment, at its commencement, ask for the light and the love that may qualify us for profitable study. Let us pray.

Almighty and most merciful God, our adorable Saviour, be present with us while we seek to receive light from Thee, and concerning Thee. We confess that we are but receivers of the instruction which Thy mercy is disposed to impart; Thou art the way, the truth, and the life. We entreat Thee so to govern our minds by the influence of Thy Holy Spirit; that in Thy light we may see light—that we may love the light we see—and that we may walk in the light, to the glory of Thy Divine name, for the salvation of our own souls, and for the happiness of those who love and fear Thee. These mercies, Almighty Lord Jesus, we ask in Thine own most sacred name, and for Thy loving kindness' sake. Amen.

THE FIRST LECTURE.

HOW TO THINK OF THE DIVINE UNITY AND TRINITY.

"And the Lord shall be King over all the earth: in that day shall there be one Lord, and His name one."—Zech. xiv. 9.

THE subject before us is one of the very highest importance. We know that by many it is esteemed to be of so mysterious a character, that the idea of knowing God, of having a clear and comprehensive view of the Holy Being we worship, is supposed to be entirely beyond our reach. And there are two general views, which certainly are not such as to give us a clear discernment of the God we are required to love. One of these views lays especial stress upon what is indeed most emphatically declared in the Scriptures—namely, "That there is one God and no more." But those who hold the idea that we have just named to the exclusion of any notion of there being a Trinity in the Divine Being, say that this one God has neither form nor image by which the mind can grasp Him. In such a case, it would seem that when the soul endeavours to fix itself upon this notion, it can only be in conformity with the idea that was written upon the altar which Paul pointed out at Athens; it still proclaims God to be an unknown God—for the mind certainly cannot form any idea of a Being to whom it can attribute no form. When it strives to grasp such a one, it finds itself, as it were, gazing upon emptiness, and grasping a shadow. Another idea that is very commonly entertained, also, is confessed by those who hold it to be exceedingly difficult of comprehension, and that is, that there are three persons in God, and that each one of these three persons is Almighty, present everywhere, and all-knowing; none is before or after the other, or greater or less than the other; each person is God and Lord by himself, but there are not three Gods, nor three Lords. Now this, although delivered in so many words, and although capable of being presented in a great variety of aspects, yet is confessed by those who entertain it to be so mysterious even to themselves, that they are painfully perplexed; and at last the mind rests only on the words, and attaches no ideas to them. All is dark, mysterious, and contradictory. The one idea takes the notion of the unity of God, but excludes the Trinity; the other idea takes the notion of the Trinity of God, but excludes the unity.

Now, the question that we wish to propose for consideration to-night is, whether there is not some other mode of viewing the subject that will enable us to grasp both doctrines of the Sacred Scriptures, and believe there is one God; but in this one God there is also a Divine Trinity of Father, Son, and Holy Spirit?

It is supposed by some who have not considered it to be a duty to obtain a clear and rational comprehension of the faith upon which their salvation rests, that such inquiries are of no consequence. But we think it essential for every one—be the faith that has been taught to him true or not—that he should re-consider it. When he is a child, he thinks as a child, and he is taught as a child; but when he becomes a man, it is the requirement of that God who gave him manly powers, that he should go over again what he has been taught. And, as those worthier animals that furnish us the greatest uses, after they have taken the food upon which they live, are made by Divine Providence to lie down in the meadow and quietly to ruminate—to chew the cud again and to prepare the food for thorough digestion—so it is in the human mind a desideratum that ought never to be neglected, that when the memory has been well furnished with instruction from childhood—the spirit should again bring up the instruction—ruminate upon it—meditate upon it—and seek to understand it. For the religious teaching which man understands, that alone remains of service in the day of trouble and adversity; and what he does not understand is like the withered leaf, or like the artificial that has been pinned upon the tree and has not grown out of it. When the storms of life come, all such will be blown away. Hence the great Saviour said, "He that receiveth the seed into good ground, is he that heareth my word, and understandeth it; which also beareth fruit, and bringeth forth, some an hundredfold, some sixty, some thirty." But when any man "heareth the word of the kingdom, and understandeth it not, then cometh the wicked one, and catcheth away that which was sown in his heart."

Let us, then, endeavour to ascertain if we can understand this foundation-stone of all theology, so that it may be so firmly fixed as to be worthy of the glorious promise given in Isaiah: "Behold, I lay in Zion for a foundation a stone, a tried stone, a precious corner-stone, a sure foundation: he that believeth shall not make haste."—Isaiah xxviii. 16. "For other foundation can no man lay than that is laid, which is Jesus Christ,"—1 Cor. iii. 11. Well, then, we have mentioned that those who have been used to hear, and have familiarised themselves with the fact that there is mention, in the New Testament at least, of Father, Son, and Holy Ghost, or as it might be better rendered, Holy Spirit.—The word "Ghost," in old times, meant the same as "Spirit" signifies now; though now it is an ugly word, and means a phantom. It is derived from the old German word Geist, and signifies that which flows out, as the spirit of truth, but afterwards it obtained a signification which did not belong to it. The spiritual person which had left the body at death was called "ghost," and hence, when the Holy Ghost is mentioned, it often suggests to the mind, not the idea of holy truth which it originally did, but the idea of a sort of ghostly personage distinct from other persons. Now it often occurs to such as have been taught beforehand, that there are three persons in the Deity, and one is called "Father," and one is called "Son," and one is called the "Holy Ghost;"—to imagine that inasmuch as they read in the New Testament the terms Father, Son, and Holy Ghost.

they have learned in the New Testament that there are three persons in God. They suppose that they can readily lay their fingers upon some text that says, "The Father is a person, the Son is a person, and the Holy Ghost is a person." But when they come really to search the Scriptures for such an object, they find, what is the fact, that nowhere, from the commencement of the first book of Revelation to the termination of the last, is there such an expression as three persons and one God, or one person of the Father, another person of the Son, and another person of the Holy Ghost. There are no such phrases to be found in the Bible. They are merely to be found in human, manufactured creeds, which were made in times that we now know were times not of intelligence, but times of much ignorance, much error, much of tyrannical pretence, and of but little real, true, intellectual light. If these creeds, therefore, have anything that is not to be found in this Divine Book, we would that none of us should be held responsible for their contents; but that we should come "to the law and to the testimony. If they speak not according to this word, it is because there is no light in them."

Our first remark then, is, that nowhere in the Sacred Scriptures can any one find a text; and if he has imagined so, let him earnestly set about it to-morrow, and not be satisfied until he has thoroughly examined that question; that nowhere in this Divine Book is there to be found any declaration that says, and we think not that means, that there are more persons in God than one. The line of teaching in the sacred volume is this: In the Old Testament it is taught that there is one God, Jehovah, and no more, and this one God would come into the world to save mankind. In the New Testament it is taught that this one God did come into the world under the name of Jesus Christ; that He was "God manifest in the flesh." This is the first point.

Secondly: That to Jesus Christ in the Scriptures is attributed the terms Father, Son, and Holy Spirit, separately and combinedly, in single declarations and in compound declarations, where all the names are grouped together. And,

Thirdly: We will endeavour to address ourselves to such fair objections as may occur to the thoughtful, duly desirous of examining this subject fully.

I. We have said then, in the first place, that the doctrine of the Old Testament is, that the one God, Jehovah himself, would come into the world to save mankind. In the New Testament it is taught that Jesus Christ, who did come into the world, was God Himself "manifest in the flesh," fulfilling the prophecies of the Old Testament.

Now, there are such remarkable declarations on both these points, that any one who fully gives himself to verify them as we present them, we conceive will be astonished that he has overlooked the plain and emphatic teaching which we have pointed out. Let us take a few instances. It is said in Isaiah xliii. 10, 11, "Before me there was no God formed, neither shall there be after me. I, even I, am the Lord (Jehovah), and beside me there is no Saviour." Now, here there is no equivocation; there is a striking, direct, and glorious utterance, that God the Eternal One had none who was formed before Him, and after Him there would also be none formed—that He was Jehovah himself; and that He would come into the world to be the Saviour of mankind. "I, even I, am the Lord; and beside me there is no Saviour." Now, if there had been another person who was or who would be a Saviour besides Him, there can be no question but he would have known of it. The same Divine being throughout the Jewish economy had always presented the same truth. Take for instance, Deuteronomy vi. 4, and you read—"Hear, O Israel: the Lord our God is one Lord." Take again, as another specimen, the numerous utterances in Isaiah xlv., where you will find, in every variety of form, the fact declared, that the same Being who was the Creator would become the Saviour. "Verily thou art a God that hidest thyself, O God of Israel the Saviour," verse 15. "There is no God else besides me. a just God and a Saviour, there is none beside me," verse 21. "Look unto me, and be ye saved, all the ends of the earth; for I am God, and there is none else," verse 22. A very common idea is to regard the first person of the Divine Trinity as a Being that required to be appeased in the work of salvation—the second person of the Divine Trinity, as the Son that came to save man from the horrors which the first had threatened to inflict upon them. These declarations, and numerous others, point out nothing of this kind, but the reverse: that the Maker of the world, the Creator of all things, was the very One that would become the Saviour. Take, again, Isaiah xliii. 25, "I, even I, am He that blotteth out thy transgressions for mine own sake, and will not remember thy sins." Thus, again, it is a great fact that the Being who denominates himself "I"—"I, even I," and declares that He is Jehovah Himself, the one glorious God of heaven and earth—is the Being that for His own sake would blot out the sins of men, and redeem them from ruin. Turn where you will, the prophets are full of this truth. Say to them that are of a fearful heart, "Be strong, fear not: behold your God will come with vengeance, even God with a recompense, He will come and save you."—Isaiah xxxv. 4. "The voice of him that crieth in the wilderness, prepare ye the way of the Lord (Jehovah), make straight in the desert a highway for our God."—xl. 3. "Behold the Lord God will come with a strong hand, and his arm shall rule for him: behold his reward is with him, and his work before Him," verse 10. "Fear not, thou worm Jacob, and ye men of Israel, I will help thee, saith the Lord (Jehovah), and thy Redeemer, the Holy One of Israel."—xli. 14. "For thy Maker is thine husband, the Lord (Jehovah) of Hosts is his name; and thy Redeemer, the Holy One of Israel, the God of the whole earth shall he be called."—liv. 5. "Yet I am the Lord thy God from the land of Egypt, and thou shalt know no god but me; for THERE IS NO SAVIOUR BESIDE ME."—Hosea xiii. 4. Can any language be stronger? Is it not declared that there is only one Saviour, and He is

Jehovah himself! Look, also, at our text. In that day there shall be one King over all the earth; "in that day there shall be one Lord (JEHOVAH), AND HIS NAME ONE."

In the New Testament you will find the same thing is taught from the very commencement of the Lord's visitation of mankind, throughout the Gospel. Take, for instance, what is said concerning the Lord's birth into the world, as a specimen—Matthew i. 21, "Thou shalt call his name JESUS; for he shall save his people from their sins." Now, if Jesus was not Jehovah, not only would this language be itself utterly inexcusable—for who can save from sin but God himself?—but why say "He shall save his people?" His people! How his people unless He made the people, and was their proper Sovereign? They are His: He was the proprietor of them; but not only so, salvation itself implies that the Being that saves must be Divine. Who of us can save ourselves, even from the slightest sin, without Divine help and power? And who if he could save himself, can save his brother? But this glorious Being was to "save His people from their sins." And yet we have already seen that it is over and over again declared in the Old Testament that there was no Saviour but one. "I, even I, am the Lord; and beside me there is no Saviour:" and if that be true, then He whose name meant Saviour—for the word Jesus is the word Saviour in Greek—and He who is declared to have had that name, because He would save His people from their sins,—must be the very one God. If these two things are true—and no Christian can dispute them—then Jehovah and Jesus must be one.

Again, we have quoted the words which Zechariah proclaimed—"In that day there shall be one Lord, and his name one"—or one Jehovah, for the word Lord is in capital letters, and perhaps it may be as well to remind some of my audience that when they find the word "Lord" in capital letters, it is "Jehovah" in the original language; and the sense will be better here if we read, "in that day there shall be one Jehovah, and his name one." Now, who was that king? There was to be one king over all the earth. The answer is given in the same chapter, where you will find it two or three times, with this appendage to it—the King, Jehovah of Hosts. "In that day," it is said; "they shall go up to worship the King, Jehovah of Hosts, and to keep the feast of tabernacles" (Zech. xiv. 16); "and whoso will not worship the King, Jehovah of Hosts, upon them there shall be no rain" (verse 17); meaning, of course, the rain of the Divine influence and blessing. In the ninth verse of the ninth chapter of the same prophecy it is brought still more markedly before us; it is said, "Shout, O daughter of Jerusalem: behold, thy King cometh unto thee: He is just, and having salvation; lowly, and riding upon an ass, and upon a colt the foal of an ass." And you will find in the Gospel that the Lord Jesus did this literally; and it is said it was done to fulfil what the prophet said, "Behold, thy King cometh unto thee," &c. (Matt. xxi. 4, 5); thus pointing out the person who would be King; and the Scripture says, "He was the one King that would be over all the earth; and in that day there shall be one Lord, and his name one." Who is the rightful Lord if Jesus Christ is not? "Ye call me Master and Lord: and ye say well; for so I am;" and the Lord says, "There shall be one Lord, and his name one."

We might go on with these parallels between the Old Testament and the New to a much greater extent, but each person can do it for himself, and it is only a general opening of the subject that we can give, thus affording hints for those who wish to know the Lord, to prosecute their inquiry until that knowledge becomes fully received in their minds. But allow me to impress upon your attention, my beloved friends, the fact that it is a grievous mistake for persons to imagine that the Lord is not a Being that can be known. On the contrary, in the Scriptures it is pointed out to be the Christian's especial privilege—the great highway to salvation—to know his God. It is said, "the knowledge of the Lord shall cover the earth, as the waters cover the sea." "To know him," it is said, "is life eternal." (John xvii. 3.) "Let not the wise man glory in his wisdom, neither let the mighty man glory in his might; let not the rich man glory in his riches: but let him that glorieth, glory in this, that he understandeth and knoweth me, that I am the Lord which exercise loving-kindness, judgment, and righteousness, in the earth." (Jer. ix. 23, 24.) Let us take hope and heart, therefore, for if we have not yet got a clear knowledge of our God; we may obtain it. Possibly it may be that some dark and dreary mode of regarding this subject may have darkened our minds; but let us determine that we will apply ourselves, that we may see this great truth, not as mystery and darkness, but as the very light of life, "I am the truth," says the Lord Jesus; let him prosecute his inquiry after the real character of the Lord Jesus Christ—"I am the way, and the truth"—and let him then open his heart to receive the Divine influence of the Saviour, and he will find that he is also the "life;" "no man cometh unto the Father but by me."

II. Let us now endeavour to advance a stage further We have declared that the names Father, Son, and Holy Spirit are all attributed in the Scriptures to Jesus Christ, and what they mean is contained in Him, and nowhere else.

Allow me, just by the way, to prevent any one supposing that the view now offered goes to ignore either the Father or the Holy Spirit. Those who have not got a clear idea—who have not given themselves patience to get a complete view of the doctrine thus manifested of the whole Divine Trinity in Jesus Christ, sometimes take away the notion that we are putting forth one person of the Trinity, and leaving the others aside. What we mean is, that the Trinity is not a Trinity of persons, but a Trinity of essential constituents. There is a Trinity in God, and that is the reason that there is a Trinity, we conceive, in everything. Throughout the whole universe you meet continually with trinities, but always in unities. Take, for instance, the sun; and the sun is perhaps the grandest emblem in material nature of that glorious Being who is called the "Sun of Righteousness," the Spiritual Sun. You have the heat of the sun, which is the grand foundation quality; the light of the sun; and you have the outflowing radiation of both: and these three are one. Take, again, any object you please: a tree. You have the essential nature of the tree; you have the outward form of the tree; and there are the fruits which the tree produces: and these three are one. Each one of these is not a tree by itself; but the whole three form a tree. Take a flower. There is its life, or essence; its form, and its fragrance: and these three are one. Take a human being, who is said to be in the image and likeness of God. You have the soul, which is the grand essential principle in man: you have the body, which is the outward form or manifestation; and then you have the works, which proceed from both together: and these three are one. If you take each part of a man it is the same. You may take the soul by itself, and you will find that there are three essential parts which form it. The whole of the activities of the soul may be classed into the volitions that belong to the *will;* the thoughts, which belong to the *intellect;* and the *power,* that flows from both of these together. Take the body. There is the head; the trunk; and the legs; and these form one human body. Take any part of the body. The skin is formed, as all acquainted with physiology will tell you, of three parts, that make it a beautiful trebled network around man; but of these three, each forms a part; and the whole three form the human skin. Take the finger, and it is divided into three joints. The arm, and there are three parts. Nay, take any object, whatever you please. A grain of dust; and there is its length, and breadth, and depth: and these three are one. You cannot get a thing at all without a trinity, and when you get the trinity, you have the whole. One quality is not a trinity: nor can it be a separate existence by itself. And so it is with the Trinity of God, from whom all other trinities have come.

The Father is the essential Divine Love in God; the very

essence from which all God's glorious attributes proceed and act. The Son is the Divine form, or manifestation of God; that which enables us to know God—to approach Him—and thus to love Him, and believe in Him. But He is not separate from the Father—the Father is in Him; "I and the Father are one." The Lord Jesus says, "The Father who is in me, He doeth the works." And hence you will find, if you examine the evidence well, that you will be struck with the fact, that there are any who look for a Father out of Jesus Christ, when we are so distinctly assured that it is not possible to approach the Father but by Jesus Christ. "God was in Christ, reconciling the world unto himself;" and that is the reason why Isaiah uses that magnificent round of Divine expressions, when speaking of God's being about to descend and save mankind, which you will find in Isaiah ix. 6, "For unto us a child is born, unto us a son is given; and the government shall be upon his shoulder; and his name shall be called Wonderful, Counsellor, The Mighty God, (not a mighty God, you perceive, because there is one, only one), The Everlasting Father, The Prince of Peace." Now really, unless we are disposed to imagine, in obedience to ancient prejudice, that there are two Fathers, one in Christ and one out of Him, it would seem that this sublime declaration ought to teach us to seek for God in Christ, for the same Being who is called "a son," and "a child," is also called "the Everlasting Father," and "the Prince of Peace." And He himself, when in the world, taught the same truth with the greatest clearness. Turn to the 14th chapter of John, and you will find such teaching as may assist to remove a little perplexity from those minds who may overlook the fact, that it is with the sun of the soul, as it is with the sun of nature—he rises gradually. Man's mental eye is like his natural eye. If light were to come in all its dazzling splendour at once, from midnight darkness, we should be very soon blinded. And so, if from the darkness of the materialism in which the world was sunk when our Saviour came, He had at once given them the full truth respecting Himself, they would have become spiritually blinded. Hence it was, that He disclosed His character to mankind gradually. When first Philip and Nathanael began to talk about Jesus, they said—"We have found Him of whom Moses, in the law and the prophets, did write—Jesus of Nazareth, the Son of Joseph."—John i. 45. They imagined that He was Joseph's son, a human being like themselves, but selected by God to be a great teacher, a grand prophet. When, however, they saw Him exert such power as no human being could possess, and exert it by His own independent will, when He was addressed by the leper to be cleansed, said, "I will, be thou clean," and the man became immediately healed; when He was addressed by those who, in that terrific storm on the sea of Galilee, imagined they were about to be overwhelmed and He had forgotten or cared not for them; when they cried out, "Lord, save us, we perish," and beheld Him rise in simple but Divine majesty, and, first of all, rebuke them for their little faith, and then utter the simple words, "Peace, be still," and all was hushed into calm and quiet, they cried out, "What manner of man is this, that even the winds and the sea obey him!" They learned then that the dignity of Him who was the Master of the raging sea was not the dignity of a mere man, but the dignity of a Divine man; and at length they gathered around Him, trembling with their surmises and anxieties, for information, and they said, "Lord, show us the Father, and it sufficeth us:" and Jesus replied, as you will find in John xiv. 9, "Have I been so long time with you, and yet hast thou not known Me, Philip? HE THAT HATH SEEN ME HATH SEEN THE FATHER, and how sayest thou, then, Show us the Father?" Can there be any teaching more solemn or more express than that? Can we imagine that when the disciples gathered around the Master, full of solicitude to be rightly understood and rightly led, He would equivocate with them? Assuredly not. They asked Him to show them the Father. Shall not we, then, receive the same reply, and ponder it deeply—impress it in our hearts, remembering that the Lord Jesus, though as to His human nature the Son, as to His Divine nature was also the " Everlasting Father and the Prince of Peace ?"

Again: In the book of Revelation, you will find another of these group passages, in the first chapter and eighth verse, where it is said, " I am Alpha and Omega (that is, taking the first and last letters of the Greek alphabet, to intimate that He was the very beginning and end of all things; as if He had said, "I am the *a* and the *z* "), the beginning and the ending of all things, who is, and who was, and who is to come, the Almighty." Here, again, can we conceive that there is any want of plainness, especially when we find the Lord Jesus adding, in the 17th verse, " Fear not, I am the first and the last?" Then you perceive that three times over He replies in what seems to be tautology, unless we bear in mind that there is a Divine Trinity, and that He is the " first and the last" of every part of the Trinity. "I am the Alpha and Omega "—as if He had said, " I am the first and last of all Divine love:" " I am the beginning and the ending "—as if He had said, " I am the first and last of all Divine wisdom and intelligence, or manifestation:" " The first and the last"—as if He had said, " I am the beginning and the ending of all Divine power," and this because, as the last expression says, " I am the Almighty." In fact, the very idea of God is included in this term, " Almighty," and it is such as that there can only be one such Being for, although there are three necessary ideas involved in it, each one implies the other, and cannot exist without it. For instance, He is the Almighty: there can be only one Almighty; for, if one person has all might, there can be no might of the same kind for any other person. If I have got possession of the whole of anything, no one else can have any of it. If another has any part I cannot have it all. " The Almighty."

Again: The idea of all-might implies two others. It implies all-knowledge; it implies presence everywhere, to know and perceive everything. No person can do everything unless he knows how to do it—no person can do anything if he is not present where it is to be done. Omnipotence, omniscience, and omnipresence go together. Again, a person cannot do all things unless he has all-knowledge. But, if he has all-knowledge and not energy of will, he also would not have all-might. Knowing how to do a thing is not sufficient. There must be the volition to do as well as the knowledge. If I had the power to build a house, if I had all the might requisite to produce a house, and I produce it, the production of the house not only proves that I had the power to do it—I knew the plans of operation, I knew where to get the materials—but I had also had the will to do it. So that you see these three things go together. So in God there are infinite might, infinite intelligence, and infinite love. Here is a Divine Trinity meeting us in three terms, but the essentials so expressed are so connected that you cannot separate them. And, therefore, when the Lord Jesus said, "All power is given unto me, in heaven and in earth," or, as I have just before quoted, that He is "the Almighty," it proves that He hath all wisdom, and that He hath all love; for these two must be in the mind of the Almighty; and He who has all power, all wisdom, and all love, must be the only God. Other beings can have no Divine wisdom, no Divine power, no Divine love; and he who has no Divine wisdom, no Divine power, no Divine love, is no God at all. So that you perceive, if we closely attend to the subject, we shall find that reason confirms the same truth that revelation teaches.

Allow me just to suggest that in all our inquiries we should be very careful not to put one kind of truth in opposition to another. There can be no opposition really between truth of different kinds. That which is really proved to be true by any one mode of thinking, must agree with all other truths. Three times three make nine, according to arithmetic, and you will find they make it

B

according to everything else; and so, if we have got the right idea of God from the Scriptures, it will harmonise with reason, it will harmonise with science, it will harmonise with fact, it will harmonise with every mode of viewing truth.

We have proved then, we conceive, that the Father and the Son are both of them attributed to our Lord Jesus Christ, and the Holy Spirit is just in the same way attributed to Him. In the same chapter in which he so clearly points out that the Father is in Him, he says, concerning the Holy Spirit, it is "The Spirit of truth, the Comforter, whom I will send unto you from the Father." And thus, perhaps, a person who did not well examine the subject, would say, "Don't you see, He says, 'I will send Him from the Father?'"—and with this idea of a Father somewhere out of Jesus Christ, and of sending in the same way that a man sends another man—a finite being sends another finite being—he has a representation in his mind of three separate individuals. But we should always bear in mind that the Father of the Sacred Scriptures is the Father in Jesus, and when he sends the Holy Spirit, he sends Him from the Father within Him —not from some Father above or below Him—and this Father, within Him, is Him, as He proceeds to explain. He says, "For he dwelleth with you, and shall be in you," (ver. 17)—that is, the Holy Spirit was Jesus, not dwelling outwardly with them, but dwelling inwardly with them when His outward presence was gone—dwelling by His holy influence with them. "He dwelleth with you, and shall be in you. I will not leave you comfortless; I will come to you." Now, here you perceive the Saviour Himself explains what it is, and that it is Himself coming unto man when the Comforter comes to man. And so, after the resurrection, you will read in John xx. 22, it is said, "Then came Jesus, the doors being shut, and stood in the midst," fulfilling what is manifest in the fact that He was that Being to whom no doors present any obstacle

—that He was that Being who can be constantly present everywhere—as He said, "Wherever two or three are gathered together in my name, there am I in the midst of them." He manifested Himself in the midst of the disciples, and said, after breathing upon them, "Receive ye the Holy Spirit." Now, does not this teach most distinctly that His Spirit was the Holy Spirit? Can any one conceive that He breathed anything else but His Divine influence upon them? And hence the Apostle Paul says, as you will find in 2 Corinthians iii. 17, "Now, the Lord is that Spirit: and where the Spirit of the Lord is, there is liberty." The Spirit is not a distinct separate person from the Lord; it is the Lord. And so in the book of Revelation, to each Church the Lord Jesus sends His divine commission. They begin by seven descriptions of Himself, taking something out of the full, perfect, and glorious form that He showed to John at first. He began each separate epistle with one of these. To one He says, "Thus saith the first and the last;" He proceeds to say to another, "Thus saith he that holdeth the seven stars;" to another, "Thus saith he that hath the seven Spirits of God." And here allow me to suggest to those who have sometimes thought, wherever they find an emblem or a form, that it means a separate individual —(as, for instance, where the dove descends on the Lord Jesus at His baptism—that it was a separate Divine person descending upon Him), that the dove is an emblem of conjunction. It is an emblem of love and wisdom combined. Thus we are told to be "wise as serpents, and harmless as doves." To show that the Divine person had this in Him infinitely and completely, the dove appeared. Jesus says, "These things saith he that hath the seven Spirits of God." If we suppose that each Spirit is a distinct or separate person, we must make seven different persons of the Holy Spirit. But it is to teach us that He possesses all the fulness of the Spirit of God. The number seven is found in Scripture wherever some thing especially blessed, full, perfect, sacred, and Divine is meant. The seven Spirits of God, like the seven stars, and like the use of the number seven, which you will find very remarkable throughout the Scriptures, is the emblem of all that is holy; and His having the seven Spirits of God, is said to teach us that the whole Spirit of God is possessed by Him; and, therefore, when He commences each epistle with something which means Himself, He concludes it in all cases by saying, "He that hath an ear to hear, let him hear what the Spirit saith unto the churches." He is the only person that has been speaking —thus teaching that when He speaks, the Spirit speaks, when He exerts His Divine influence, it is the influence of the Divine Spirit which is exerted. A man's spirit is not a different person from himself, and God's Spirit is not a different person from God himself. Jesus said, again, as you will read in the sixteenth verse of the last chapter of Revelation, "I, Jesus, am the root and the offspring of David, and the bright and morning star." He is the "root," because He is the Father, from whom all things spring; He is the "offspring," because He has assumed the human nature by which God manifested himself; and He is the "bright and morning star," because He is the glorious Spirit that illuminates man, when he turns in the night time of sin and folly, and brings to the new day, from which the light of heaven shines over his soul. Jesus is the "All in all."

Such, then, are some of the evidences upon which, if we dwell, we conceive there will be no reason to hesitate to accept the glorious fact presented by the prophets, realised in the Gospels, proclaimed by the apostles. Paul said, "In him (Christ) dwelleth all the fulness of the Godhead bodily."—Col. ii. 9. "Ye are complete in him, who is the 'he' of all principality and power,"—v. 10. "In him dwelleth all the fulness of the Godhead bodily"—love, wisdom, power, righteousness, justice—everything that belongs to the nature of the Godhead, all dwells bodily in Jesus Christ. "In him dwelleth all the fulness of the Godhead bodily;" and hence Paul says, again, when speaking to the Romans, as you will find in Romans ix. 6, "Of whom Christ came, who is over all, God blessed for ever,"—who is not a second person, who is not an inferior dignity, but "who is over all," and not only over all, but over all, "God," whom all the angels worship, Heb. i. 6, to whom every knee should bow, "God blessed for ever." Peter said, "Jesus Christ is Lord of all,"—Acts x. 36. John said, "This is the True God and Eternal Life,"—1 John v. 20; while Jude concludes with the grand doxology, "To the only wise God, our Saviour, be glory and majesty, dominion and power, both now and for ever."—v. 25. When this great truth is illuminated by other truths, which tend to open the mind to "all the fulness of the Godhead," each portion will fall into its right place, and give to us a knowledge of God, which we can give to others. Let us all hope and pray that the time may come when this glorious God our Saviour can be approached, not in the way of something mysterious, which we cannot understand, but as the "Bread of Life," the "Light of Life," the power that can quicken our souls unto salvation—when this glorious Saviour may be preached over all the earth, and the "knowledge of the Lord,"—not the perplexities and mysteries of the Lord, but "the knowledge of the Lord shall cover the earth, as the waters cover the sea."

But an inquirer may object that Christ is said to be sent by God, and how can He be God Himself? It is a very proper question, How He can be God Himself, if God sent Him? But certainly it ought not to be proposed as an objection, unless, first of all, we ignore the fact that He was "God manifest in the flesh." If He was "Immanuel, God with us," why He was God Himself; and although it is right for us to ask HOW He could be sent from God, it is hardly right, when we have just admitted that He was God Himself, to object that He was not God Himself—that He was some one else. It is merely advancing two opposite sides on the same question. But the fallacy is here:—We are supposing (and here originate many of the mistakes which persons have upon this subject), we are supposing that we have to do with a finite being—with a being who is located just in one place, and nowhere else: and hence persons will say, "If Christ was God Himself, what were they doing in heaven when He was upon earth?"—forgetting that He is the Being who fills heaven and earth. We all admit that Christ is wherever His faithful followers are. —"Where two or three are gathered together in my name, there am I in the midst of them." But is not He in heaven also? We should never forget that the Being we are talking about, is the Being who said, "Am I not a God at hand, and not a God afar off? Do not I fill heaven and earth?" Jesus Christ said He was in heaven, when He was upon the earth, as you will read in John iii. 13, "And no man hath ascended up to heaven, but He that came down from heaven, even the Son of Man, which is in heaven." Was not this at the same time as He was talking to them upon the earth? What, then, does descending mean? It means this. We regard God as a great way off; because He is invisible to us, we are not aware of His presence; we think He is very far off, because we cannot see Him; and when God manifests Himself, it seems to us as if He was sent down from where He was, to where He is. This is merely an appearance. It does not belong to God Himself. When He made Himself visible, it is called sending into the world. It was not another person that sent Him, it was Himself that sent Him. Just read John xii. 45, and you will find there is this simple declaration—"And he that seeth me, seeth Him that sent me." That is the Saviour's own answer to the question. It was His own love that brought Him into the world; it was His own desire to save mankind; it was His own affection and pity for men that led Him, who was the Eternal God, to descend as a man and a brother, to help, and to save, and to bless us. "He that seeth me, seeth Him that sent me."

But others may say, "Well, there are Father, Son, and Holy Ghost mentioned in the Scriptures. When Christ commanded us to go out to baptize, He said, "Go ye therefore and teach all nations, baptizing them in the name of the Father, and of the Son, and of the Holy Ghost; teaching them to observe whatsoever I have commanded you; and, lo, I am with you alway, even unto the end of the world." We teach that there is in God, the Father, the Son, and the Holy Spirit, but it is all in the Saviour. Just notice that remark, "baptizing them in the name"—not names—"in the name of the Father, and of the Son, and of the Holy Ghost." This teaches us that there is one name only, the name of the Father and of the Son and of the Holy Spirit. And what name is that? It is the name of Jesus Christ; and, therefore, you will read in the Acts of the Apostles, when they baptized, they baptized in the name of Jesus. Take, for instance, the fifth verse of the nineteenth chapter of the Acts, and you will find "they baptized them in the name of the Lord Jesus." They surely understood their Divine Master. He told them to go and baptize in the name of the "Father, and of the Son, and of the Holy Spirit," and they went and baptized in the name of the "Lord Jesus." Why so? Because Jesus is the name of the Father, the Son, and the Holy Spirit, just as the name of each of us is the name of the soul, and body, and works—it is the name of the whole man. Just notice the beginning and end of that command. The beginning of it is in the verse immediately coming before,—"All power is given unto Me in heaven and in earth." Then perhaps some one may say, "Jesus says given!" Who is the giver? "All power is given unto me;" well, but who is the giver? You suppose the Father, perhaps, separate from Jesus; but if it is a Father separate from Jesus, you will find that it is a Father whom we have nothing to do with. He has given up all power. Besides, if all power was given to Jesus by a person separate from Himself, before Jesus had the power He was not God. A Divine person with no power is not God in any way. And after the Father gave all power to Jesus, if the Father was a separate person from Jesus, the Father would have no power, because He had given it all away. We therefore could have no need whatever to look to a Divine person that had no power— that had given it away—resigned it. When we pray to a God, we pray to one whom we believe has power to help us, and if He was separate from Jesus, He would have no power to help us at all; no—all power was given to Jesus; just in the same way as the soul of each man gives to his body the power to talk, and walk, and act. Not as a separate person giving away from himself to another person, but as the inward Divine Love giving to His Humanity all its capabilities to save, and love, and bless mankind. "The Father who is in me, He doeth the works."—John xiv. x. Well, then the Lord Jesus says, as if to teach us that His Humanity was now the grand medium by which the essential Deity would deal with mankind, and teach and rule the Church and bless the universe, "All power is given unto me." God brought Himself nigh by taking human nature, and in that human nature approached to save and bless mankind. And not only does the Saviour say this, but He says, "Therefore," that was because all power was His—"Therefore, go and teach all nations, baptizing them into the name of the Father, and of the Son, and of the Holy Spirit. If these things were not in the Lord Jesus, there would be no connection with what had gone before, because He said all power was given unto Him. If He was one of these, and all power was given to that one, what would be the meaning of baptizing in the name of the other two that had no power? So that you see the commencement of the passage in reality teaches the same truth, that the Father, Son, and Holy Spirit are in the Lord Jesus; and He adds in concluding, "And, lo, I am with you alway." If there were three separate persons. why not say, "We will be with you alway?" On this account alone, He is "King of kings, and Lord of lords;"

not by any separate usurped authority, but because the whole Godhead is in Him.

"Jesus prayed to the Father." This also is an objection felt by many persons, perhaps by all at first. If the Father and Jesus were really one, what is meant by His praying to the Father? There is not yet in the mind of those who feel that objection a knowledge of the work of redemption, and how that glorious work was performed. Jesus took our nature, and was in all respects tempted like as we are. He took our nature upon Him that He might conquer our spiritual foes; and He glorified it by the same process by which He regenerates ours. That He might go through all the states through which we go; and lead us and teach us in all things was one of His great purposes in the incarnation. He led us in the work of regeneration, and, first sanctifying His own assumed humanity, He gives us power to sanctify our own.

Now, when we are going through the work of regeneration, our experience tells us we have a divided manhood; we are the same as if we had two men within us, the new man with new hopes and new feelings, and the old man with his old temper and his old opposition to everything good and right. And, when we go, deeply into trials and temptations, it seems very distinctly as if we had two different persons struggling within us. If what we think when these states were going on were written down, there would be a dialogue as complete as if it took place between two separate individuals struggling together for the mastery. Therefore, you will find that in some parts of the Scripture holy writers address their souls. For instance, the Psalmist said, "Why art thou cast down, O my soul? and why art thou disquieted in me?" And so the Apostle Paul speaks, when at the end of the seventh chapter of Romans he says, "I delight in the law of God after the inward man, but there is another law in my members warring against the law of my mind," and he cries out, "O wretched man that I am! who shall deliver me from the body of this death?"—v. 22-24. Every person who has entered into the struggles of this passage of life's history, of this campaign over which we have to go if we become fit for heaven, must have seen in his experience this double character of the human soul. Now, the Lord Jesus Christ went through precisely the same state as to kind, but with Him it was far more severe than with us. He had all hell against Him. He trod the winepress alone, and in the terrible hours of His struggle, when He was sustaining the powers of darkness for us (mind the difference between Him and us; He overcame alone, we overcome by power from Him). We overcome in our little struggles, because He gives us power to tread upon serpents and scorpions.—Luke x. 19. But He overcame by His own power, and He says, "For their sakes I sanctify myself, that they also might be sanctified through the truth." He had first to do this glorious work subduing hell; of glorifying, perfecting His human nature by His own power within; and when He cried to the Father, it was to the Father within Him. Just as, when we are in trial, we oftentimes summon our faith, our former love, our firmness, our courage, we look inwardly for the excellencies and virtues we have before felt within. And although we seem as if all was gone from us, yet when we look up or look inward, and pray for hope and faith and love to descend and help us, these come down, not as separate persons, but as principles in a higher degree of the soul, and when they descend by power from God, we have obtained the victory, and we go on conquering and to conquer. At last we come into a state in which from being double-minded we become of one mind from head to foot, a whole man brought into the image of our God and Saviour. Our two-foldness lasts for a time only, and then is lost in unity; so with the Lord. In His struggles he was two, in His triumphs He became one. And, when He had fully perfected His human nature, there was no longer any praying to the Father; all that was finished, and He said, "I am the first and last; I cast out evils, and I do cures to-day and to-morrow, and the third day I shall be perfected." He became perfected, and division existed no longer. Thus it is that these things belong to the state of His humiliation; all the time while He was going through the changes to redeem mankind, He was not in His permanent state. Now, He reigns upon the throne of heaven—God and Christ, in one glorious Divine person, the only Ruler of heaven and earth.

Hence, therefore, we see that by this view we arrive at the fulfilment of what is declared in John xiv. 26, when Jesus said, "The time cometh when I will no more speak unto you in proverbs, but I will show you plainly of the Father;"—the time of the seventh trumpet, announced in the Book of Revelation, when John said, "And there were great voices in heaven, saying, The kingdoms of this world are become the kingdoms of our Lord, and of his Christ, and He"—not they, as if they were two separate individuals, but "He," Lord and Christ, in one glorious person—"He shall reign for ever and ever."

Let us, then, enter upon the examination of this glorious truth. If we have had any perplexity about the Being we ought to worship—if we have had any mysterious cloud hanging over us, as to whether we ought to look up to an unknown God, or how we ought to direct the eye of faith, and the heart of love, so as to adore Him with all the heart, let us come to the Saviour God. Let us hear Him saying, "Come unto me;" "Abide in me." And approach His own glorious Divine person, and we shall find that He will do all for us which the soul requires, either of light, or life, or power. He will give us the victory over our sins; He will give us peace and comfort in our dying hour; and when eternity opens upon us, we shall find that He is there with His angels to bless us, and say, "I will give thee the crown of life." With this one glorious "Sun of righteousness" shining in our mental and spiritual system, we shall find that in all our walk, we have had God with us, who shows that He not only loves us, but will not spare anything that is requisite for our safety and salvation. God, who can "save to the uttermost," and show that there was nothing that infinite love and wisdom could do that He was not prepared to do—was God who descended upon earth "to seek and to save that which was lost;" and He will seek, and save, and bless us. To Him, therefore, be glory and dominion for ever.

At the conclusion of the lecture, Dr. Bayley intimated his willingness to answer any question or objection that might be urged, and consequently a gentleman in the body of the room wished for the prayer to be explained, which Christ uttered upon the cross, namely—"My God, my God, why hast Thou forsaken me?"—and to have a reason why it was uttered.

Dr. BAYLEY said: Our friend has presented the most striking example which exists in the Scriptures, on a small scale, of prayer to the Father; and it is that point in the Saviour's experience which is paralleled in the deepest depths of man's experience in his trials. There are periods when, in man's case, he seems to be so completely shut up in darkness and despair that he thinks, as appeared to the Saviour, that all hope is gone, and that he is forsaken by all. Now the Saviour, in going through all that man has to go through, realised this; His Humanity was apparently left to itself. It was the Humanity that prayed, not a separate Divine person; and the Humanity shrouded in darkness, in this depth of the despairing trial that all hell brought upon Him; at this time, the Humanity, in order to show that salvation was from the Divinity within, said, "My God, my God, why hast Thou forsaken me?" God seemed to have forsaken Him, but it was not really so; it is not a real fact that God ever forsakes us, or forsook *His own Humanity*, but it seems to us as if He does, and we speak according as it seems to us to be. He did not forsake Daniel when he was in the den of lions; and the Divinity did not forsake the Humanity on that dreadful trial on the cross. But the point to be borne in mind is, that it was the Human which seemed to be forsaken of the inner Divine, but both Human and Divine belonged to the *same sacred person*. Therefore our Lord, in explaining this beforehand, as you will find in John x. 18, said, "No man taketh it (my life) from me, but I lay it down of myself. I have power to lay it down, and I have power to take it again." The life that was laid down was in the suffering Humanity that appeared to be forsaken, and that uttered the cry, in order to show that it experienced all that we experience, but in a greater degree. He says as to His inmost degree of the Humanity, "No man taketh it from me. I have power to lay it down, and I have power to take it again." The life laid down is the suffering Human, I which laid it down is the Divine Human within. The Father is expressive of the inmost infinite love, from which all power comes. "The Father, who is in me, He doeth the works." So that if we only bear this in mind, we shall find that all the duality that is spoken of in reference to the Saviour, is imaged by the duality which is experienced in us when going through states of suffering and trial. But when these states are over, there is no longer the same duality; our consciousness is no longer as of two, but the two degrees are so united that the mind becomes one from first to last—no more doubt, no more separation. So was it with the Saviour; when this great work was accomplished, and the humanity itself was glorified and made perfect, then He said, "I am the first and the last." It is called the glorification of the Son, that we might look and find in Him "all the fulness of the Godhead bodily." Now this is the explanation afforded by the New Jerusalem Church, and it appears to us complete and satisfactory. If any one has been accustomed to think this prayer a proof that there are two Divine persons, let him consider it, and dwell upon it in that point of view. How could what is Divine cry, "My God, my God, why hast Thou forsaken me?"—Shall we take up the rhapsody of Wesley, and say,

The ALMIGHTY faints beneath His load,
Dies the IMMORTAL Son of God.

Could an infinite person be overcome of pain? Besides, how uncalled for is the idea that He called to another person, and not to His own Divinity. If He was God at all, and those who make the objection generally admit that He was, He simply appeals to God, and it is a most violent assumption that He passed by his own Godhead, to appeal to another, above, and out of Himself. He simply says, My God, why hast Thou forsaken me, as David said, "My soul, why art thou disquieted within me?" David and his soul, though at the time double in consciousness, are only one human person. The Divinity and the humanity, though double in consciousness while anything human was unglorified, yet were only ONE DIVINE HUMAN PERSON. To show that the suffering part was not Divine, was one object of this exclamation. Of course, these things require thought; there are difficulties on every subject. In every science there are difficulties that meet the inexperienced. But what we would earnestly place before you is, that with this view, the difficulties are not insuperable, can be explained, and when explained, open to the mind the most beautiful, the most salutary and heavenly wisdom. If there be any friend that would like to present another view, we should be very happy to hear him; and allow me to say also that we presume to take no one by storm, all that we profess to do is to state our own views and convictions, which seem to us to be fully clear and competent to everything the soul requires, to offer them in a spirit of affection, to hear every objection that is offered in the same spirit, and thus to assist, if possible, any of our brothers and sisters that are walking on in the heavenly path. But let no one imagine that he will be treated with sarcasm or unkindness. We will give the best explanation we can, and each person can accept it or leave it, as 's conscience dictates.

Another gentleman said, "The greatest difficulty I see to

the view of the New Church, is the first verse of John. 'In the beginning was the Word, and the Word was with God, and the Word was God.'"

Dr. BAYLEY replied, "The difficulty will vanish if you remember that the Word, or *Logos*, means the Divine Wisdom. It is called afterwards "the true Light, which enlighteneth every man that cometh into the world," v. 9. Now the Word by which the heavens were made is the veriest power in the universe. The inmost Light flowing from the inmost Divine Love of the Lord. It is that in God which answers to the inmost reason of man. It was from eternity with God, but not as with another person, but as reason is with a man, that is, so as to be the man. So with the Lord. The Word was with Him, so as to be Him, and, therefore, the verse concludes, and 'THE WORD WAS GOD.'"

Another gentleman rose and said, "He spoke only for information; but if the Humanity of the Lord was the Son, how were we to understand the words of the Apostle in the Hebrews, chap. i. v. 2, 'Hath in these last days spoken unto us by his Son, whom he hath appointed heir of all things, by whom also he hath made the worlds; who being the brightness of his glory, and the express image of his person, and upholding all things by the word of his power, when he had by himself purged our sins, sat down on the right hand of the majesty on high'?"

The LECTURER replied; "The Word, which we have just seen, means the Divine Wisdom, and which the Apostle here calls, 'the brightness of his glory, and the express image of his person,' or, as it ought to be translated, 'the character of his substance,' meaning the very glow of the Divine Love; this was it which made and which sustains all worlds, not as another person, but as Jehovah Himself, putting forth His Divine energies, 'upholding all things by the Word of His power' 'Thus saith the Lord (Jehovah) thy Redeemer, and He that formed thee from the womb, I am the Lord (Jehovah) that maketh all things: that stretched forth the heavens ALONE that spreadeth abroad the heavens

BY MYSELF.'—Isa. xliv. 24. In creation there was no other person with Jehovah. He did it alone by Himself. But He did it by His Divine Truth, which is the Source of all power, and under the name of the laws of nature, governs all the worlds of matter and of mind. This Word became incarnate in the Lord. 'The Word was made flesh,'—John i. 14, and then was called the Son. 'That Holy Thing which shall be born of thee shall be called the Son of God.' The Word was not strictly the Son until it became embodied in the Humanity, yet, inasmuch as it was the Word, THE DIVINE WISDOM, the very power by which the universe was made, which became the Son, the Apostle calls the Old Testament principle by a New Testament name. When he says 'the Son made the worlds,' he means that the Divine Truth which in time became the Son did so."

Another referred to John xvii. 5. "And now, O Father, glorify thou me with thine own self, with the glory I had with thee before the world was."

The LECTURER replied, "The subject treated of, in these words, is the glorification of the Humanity of the Lord. And this was done by a similar order to that in which the Lord regenerates or spiritualizes man. Now we receive truth first, and sigh and pray that goodness may descend also, and make us perfect in love. So with the Lord's Humanity, the Eternal Divine Truth descended into it and filled it first, and inspired this prayer for the Divine Love to descend also, and thus make it fully glorified. The Divine Truth had been with the Father the Divine Love inwardly, and now sought to be conjoined with the Divine Love in the entire Humanity, and thus to be made glorious by it. It would thus become in the Human one with the Father's own self, and there would no longer be a sense of separation, but He could say, 'I and the Father are one.'—John x. 20. 'All things that the Father hath are mine.'—John xvi. 15; xvii. 10.'"

Another gentleman wished to have the passage explained, 'ouch me not, for I am not yet ascended to my Father

but go to my brethren, and say unto them, I ascend unto my Father and your Father: and to my God and your God."
—John xx. 17.

Dr. BAYLEY desired the gentleman to dismiss from his mind the idea of space in relation to this subject, as if the Father were a great height up away from the Son. The Son had not to ascend in space, but in state. There was not yet a full and entire union in every particular of the Humanity with the Divine Love. He was arranging the things in the world of spirits, and that He might yet remain in that world He restrained the full external descent of His Divine Love. When the Divine Humanity would appear, not as Truth teaching, but as Love shining in all the fulness of Divine Glory, this was to ascend to the Father, and was shortly to take place. Mary was forbidden to touch Him until He had ascended, because she was the representative of those exalted members of the Church, who love Him intensely, with all their hearts. They are taught first to view Him as one with the Father, and then worship Him. Thomas is the representative of those who are of lower states of mind: who think naturally, and are more affected by a crucified Lord than by a glorified one. Thomas may touch Him in His unglorified state, but Mary not.

One wished to know what was meant by "Let us make man," in Genesis i. 26.

The LECTURER replied "It means that God acts through ministries. The making of man is not the forming of his body, but the elevation of his mind, so that it may come into the image and likeness of the Divine love and wisdom. This is always done by the ministry of angels, and so God says, 'Let us make man.' But, to show that God alone works in and by them as the prime mover, He says, in the next verse, 'So God created man in His own image, in the image of God created He him, male and female created He them.' Man, too, it should be borne in mind is not in the image of three persons in any way considered, he is composed of three essential parts, in one person and that is the image of God."

What is meant by Jesus saying, "And in that day ye shall ask me nothing. Verily, verily, I say unto you, whatsoever ye shall ask the Father in my name, He will give it you."—John xvi. 23.

By that day is meant His second coming, when He would reveal His true character perfectly and completely, as God the Father in a Divine Human form. The character He then held in their estimation was that of an extraordinary man, with authority and power from the Infinite Father, but not the Father Himself. He was to them a messenger from the Father, but the Father Himself was still the dark and distant God. They asked Him everything as a separate person, who had power with the Father. They could not yet think it possible that the Father Himself was there in the person of the Son. No man knew the Son but the Father, neither knew any man the Father save the Son.—Matt. xi. 27. In reality, they neither knew the Son nor the Father.—John viii. 19. When they knew the Son truly they would know the Father truly, and they would then know that Jesus was the Father in a Divine human form. They would no longer know Him in the character of a separate Son, but they would know Him as the revealed Father. They would ask Him nothing as a messenger from the Father, but they would ask him everything as the Father Himself. They would ask Him nothing as the Father's friend, but they would ask Him everything as the Father in person. At that time they would know that He did not pray to the Father for them. "I say not unto you that I will pray the Father for you,"—xvi. 26; but that, as the Father Himself, He loved them,—ver. 27, and whatsoever they prayed for in His name, in His Spirit He would do it for them.—John xiv. 14. The passage, therefore, refers to the change of state in man, when he learns and feels that—

> He, who on earth as man was known,
> And felt our woes and pains,
> Now seated on the eternal throne,
> The God of glory reigns.

Question. Does it not appear that we are one with Christ, as He is one with the Father, from what He says, John xvii., "That they may be one, even as we are." And thus His oneness with the Father is not a personal union, no more than our oneness with Him is a personal union.

Answer. The Lord's teaching is, that He is the soul of His kingdom in heaven and the Church, and the Father is His soul. "I in them," He says, "and thou in me, that they may be made perfect in one."—ver. 23. Unless, however, He were an infinite person, He could not be in all the members of His Church in heaven and on earth perfecting them. He is the vine, we are the branches, and the Father is in Him; and the Father and the Son are so closely united, that when we are in the Son we are in the Father also—and such an union, such an entire oneness, so that wherever the Son is the Father is, could only be the most perfect—that is, a personal union. Hence He says, "That they also may be one in us."

Q. What does Paul mean by saying that, at the end, the Son shall deliver up the kingdom to God, even the Father, when He shall have put down all rule, and all authority and power?

He does not mean that there will be an absolute change in the ruler of the Church, but that the Church will change her ideas about Him. In the old dispensation, the Lord Jesus has ruled only as a mediator, a Son under the Father; but, in the New Dispensation He will rule as the everlasting Father and the Prince of Peace. It will still be Jesus in a new character, for He is all in all. Hence, absolutely, the Lord Jesus is, and ever will be, the Sovereign in His Church, for He is the King of kings, and Lord of lords.—Rev. xix. 16. "Of the increase of His government and peace there shall be no end."—Isa. xi. 7. "His dominion is an everlasting dominion, which shall not pass away, and His kingdom that which shall not be destroyed."—Dan. vii. 14. "He shall reign for ever and ever."—Rev. xi. 15.

Q. If the Father and the Saviour are one person,

how is it that in the Epistles their names are so often separated by the conjunction and, such as God and Christ, the Father and our Lord Jesus Christ?

A. Partly, because the Father and the Saviour are two characters though not two persons. You admit that God and the Father are one person, and yet you will often find the conjunction, and, occurring between these two names. As, for instance, "Now God Himself, and our Father, and our Lord Jesus Christ direct our way unto you." —1 Thess. iii. 11. "Blessed be the God and Father of our Lord Jesus Christ."—1 Peter i. 3. It must be confessed however, that this appearance of distinction would not be so strong in many instances if we had a translation of the New Testament more rigidly exact to the original than we at present have. Thus in the new translation of the American Bible Society, there is a great improvement. For instance, in 2 Peter vii. 1, "Through the righteousness of God and our Lord Jesus Christ," is corrected, and we read, "Through the righteousness of our God and Lord Jesus Christ." Again, "Through the knowledge of God, and of Jesus our Lord"—verse 2, is given more correctly, "Through the knowledge of Jesus, our God and Lord." Again, "Looking for that blessed hope, and the glorious appearing of the great God and our Saviour Jesus Christ," is rendered "Looking for that blessed hope, and the glorious appearing of Jesus Christ our great God and Saviour."—Titus ii. 13.

At the close of the replies the Lecturer was much applauded, and no other difficulty being presented, the meeting separated.

THE SECOND LECTURE.

THE ATONEMENT, OR RECONCILIATION.

"To wit, that God was in Christ, reconciling the world unto Himself, not imputing their trespasses unto them: and hath committed unto us the word of reconciliation."—2 Cor. v. 19.

PRAYER BEFORE THE LECTURE.

ALMIGHTY and Ever-Merciful Lord, who wast manifested in the flesh to save us from our sins, be present with us, and bless us with Thy counsels. Thou art the way, the truth, and the life; be to us the way of knowledge, the truth of salvation, the life of the soul. Help us, O Saviour, to adore Thee as our Father, who in His love and in His pity did redeem us. Give us grace to understand Thy life, Thy death, and Thy glorification; and O grant that we may ever remember that, having sanctified Thyself and redeemed the world, Thou wilt redeem and sanctify us. Conquer every sinful feeling, lust, and passion, and conform us entirely to Thy blessed will. Thus prepare us for Thine everlasting kingdom. These mercies we seek in Thy blessed name, O Jesus, the Father, the Son, and the Holy Spirit, and for Thy loving-kindness sake. *Amen.*

IN advancing to the consideration of this important subject, we would, first of all, clearly define what is meant by the Atonement. It is a word made up of three distinct syllables, at-one-ment—the latter part of the word being formed from the Latin *mens*, the mind, and, consequently, the word signifies *at one mind.* This doctrine takes into consideration that God and man—owing to man's having fallen from the state in which God created him, and intended him to live and advance in—have become of two minds. Man departed from communion with God's goodness and wisdom, and sunk into a state of evil and falsehood.

which, in the Scriptures, is meant by death. "To be carnally minded," the Apostle says, "is death; but to be spiritually minded is life and peace." This state of things commenced with the fall—increased with each transgression as men continued to fall, because they continued to sin. There was no possibility of bringing these two parties, God and man, who had become of two minds, into communion, so as to make them of one mind again, but by the work of our Lord Jesus Christ, in "reconciling the world unto Himself." "God was in Christ, reconciling the world unto Himself." This reconciliation is the Atonement, and the doctrine upon the subject is the doctrine of Atonement, or at-one-ment, or agreement, or reconciliation.

Now, in the first place, I would endeavour to enforce upon my hearers that they should never forget, in all their considerations of religious subjects, these great principles, God is Love, God is One, and God is Unchangeable.

These three are all of them distinctly expressed, both in the Scriptures and in all God's works; in creation, redemption, and providence. If we search the language of the sacred volume—we may take, for instance, the beautiful description of the Apostle John, in the fourth chapter of the first epistle, and sixteenth verse. You will find it distinctly expressed thus, "God is love; and he that dwelleth in love dwelleth in God, and God in him," or, as in the 8th verse, "He that loveth not, knoweth not God, for God is love." If we advert to other parts of the sacred Scriptures, we shall find the same truth expressed, perhaps in different language, but quite as emphatically, "The Lord is good to all, and His tender mercies are over all His works."—Ps. cxliv. 9. And if we look at these works themselves, if we either regard creation on the grand scale, the universe around, or if we look at our own little world—at all the powers we possess in body and mind—at all the Divine care that has been around us from our birth up to the present moment, we see illustrated in all things this great truth, "God is love." How could any of us have been here and enjoying the blessings of life and health, notwithstanding our shortcomings, our rebellions, our forgetfulness, our incapability of adding anything to Him, or paying for the slightest comfort we receive, to say nothing of the millions of millions of blessings we are enjoying, and have enjoyed here, but that God is love? It could only be from this glorious principle that creation had its being, or that it is sustained in being; for if we imagine any other idea, any other principle, we shall find the supposition is absurd. God is love, is creation's only key. God in creation could not have sought any selfish gratification, any addition for Himself, because throughout eternity He has been the possessor of all things. Our hymns, our praises, our offerings, add nothing to His glory or renown. They are good for us, and He appoints them because they do us good. Whatever we have is derived from Him; and we add nothing to His bliss. He could not therefore have had a selfish desire in creation, and the common notion that He created all things for His own glory is worthy of fallen man, but not of the God of love. Much less could He have had an evil desire in creation, for all our powers tend to make us happy. It is only man's perversion of God's gifts that makes him miserable. There is no part, from the hair of the head to the sole of the foot of man, but what in its natural and orderly condition tends to wellbeing and bliss; and it could not be from any other purpose, therefore, than from the desire of infinite love to bless His creatures that these were made. Possessed in Himself of happiness complete, and desiring to create ever-increasing multitudes in His own image and likeness—desiring from affection to form beings such as we are, that is to say, each one of us a little universe of wants, compounds of desires and demands, that from His own fulness He might give us what we want, and bless us thereby. He made the eye that it may be delighted with the glorious scenery with which He adorns the world. He created the ear with its delights of harmony, in order that, from the majestic thunder to the feeblest music of the tiniest bird, all sounds might give us harmony and bliss. He has created the tongue, with its taste and sense of savours, in order that by all the fruits, by all the varieties of human food, with their delicate delights, and with all that constitutes their sufficiency for human taste, God might bless us again by that organ: and so throughout our whole being—from the meanest of the delights that the animal nature enjoys, to the sublimest desires that the soul has for knowledge, for wisdom, and for the highest love of God—men are in such way created that God may bless them with satisfactions, and make them happy here, and then happy through eternity hereafter. Well, a Being who has done this, we cannot suppose for a moment can be other than Infinite Love. Not loving simply, but LOVE ITSELF; and for " His pleasure all things in heaven and earth are and were created."—Rev. iv. 11.

If this be really true, the more deeply and profoundly we impress it upon our hearts, the better shall we understand all the rest of true religious teaching. Let us never forget, then, these three points—" God is love," God is one, and God is unchangeable. " I am the Lord, I change not; therefore ye sons of Jacob are not consumed."—Mal. iii. 9.

Last evening I endeavoured, as completely as the time would admit, to point out that a true idea of the Divine Trinity does not in the slightest degree impair the idea that God is one; for the Trinity consists of the infinite Love of God understood by the Father, the manifestation of God understood by the Son, who is His Wisdom, or Logos before the incarnation, and after it His Divine Form, such as made God known in heaven and on earth; and, lastly, the Spirit, outflowing from God, meant by the Holy Ghost, and all these are in the Lord Jesus Christ. He therefore who wishes to find God must come to Jesus Christ, "in Him dwells all the fulness of the Godhead bodily; " and it is impossible to see, or know, or understand the Father but in Him. John said, " No man hath seen God at any time, the only begotten Son, who is in the bosom of the Father, He hath declared Him."—John iv. 18. Jesus said, " Ye have neither heard His (the Father's) voice at any time, nor seen his shape."—John v. 37. "I am the Way, the Truth, and the Life. No man cometh unto the Father, but by me."—John xiv. 6. When, therefore, a person would have a true and clear and certain idea of the God he loves and worships, let him go with all his heart, and seek it in the knowledge and love of the Lord Jesus Christ.

But the doctrine of the Atonement, as we have said before, is the doctrine which turns our attention to that state and period when man rebelled against his Maker—violated the Divine admonition, "in the day that thou eatest thereof thou shalt surely die." Then, some have imagined, God became angry and indisposed longer to make man happy, because he had become disobedient. But the view that we conceive is taught in the Sacred Scriptures in harmony with the three grand points upon which we have dwelt is, that although man suffered loss of light, loss of happiness, loss of power for good, and loss of communication with God, and of that spiritual-mindedness which is called life, and sunk into sin and thence into sorrow, God still continued the same. Man changed, but God did not change, because He is unchangeable. He followed man with His care, with His kindness, with His messengers, with His Word, with His teaching, with angels, and with prophets, and, at length, He Himself became a man upon the earth, under the name of Jesus Christ, in order that He might save man from sin and sorrow. Hear our text, "God was in Christ reconciling the world unto Himself." Now, mark this, in Scripture not a word is ever said about Christ reconciling His Father TO US, not one word. It is always He reconciled us. Let me entreat you to hear the express language. We are exceedingly jealous that the God of love should not be misrepresented as a God of wrath and vengeance in the very arena where the infinite wonders of His love were brought to view. "For if when we were enemies WE WERE RECONCILED to God by the death of His Son, much more being reconciled we shall be saved by His life."—Rom. vi. 10. Our nature was re conciled first in Him by His death, when all imperfection was removed, and His humanity became infinitely perfect and the Head of all things, the everlasting Mediator to us.—Col. i. 17, 18; ii. 10; 1 Tim. ii. 5. See again the Epistle to the Ephesians. For He is our peace, who hath made both one, and hath broken down the middle wall of partition, having abolished IN HIS FLESH the enmity, the law of commandments in ordinances, for to make IN HIMSELF of twain one new man, that He might reconcile both UNTO God in one body by the cross, having slain the enmity thereby, or, according to the marginal and more correct reading, having slain the enmity IN HIMSELF.—Eph. ii. 15, 16. Still it is reconciling us, both Jew and Gentile, to God. And this He did by destroying in Himself the enmity of our common nature. Again, "For it pleased the Father that in Him should all fulness dwell, and having made peace through the blood of His cross, by Him to reconcile all things UNTO HIMSELF; by Him, I say, whether they be things in earth or things in heaven."—Col. i. 19, 20. "And you that were sometime alienated and enemies in your mind by wicked works, yet now hath He reconciled," verse 21. So is it ever, God RECONCILING us, not having Himself to be reconciled. "Behold the Lamb of God that taketh away the sins of the world."—John i. 29. "Thou shalt call His name Jesus, for He shall save His people from their sins."—Matt. i. 21. "Looking for that blessed hope, and the glorious appearing of the great God and our Saviour, Jesus Christ, who gave Himself for us, that He might REDEEM us from all iniquity, and purify unto Himself a peculiar people, zealous of good works."—Titus ii. 13, 14.

This is a great fact; let us not forget it. It is not, as the old theologians stated, that Christ died to reconcile the Father to us, but, as our text says, "God was in Christ reconciling the world unto Himself." In order to effect an atonement, or a reconciliation between man and Himself, his Creator came upon earth—God that made the world became our Redeemer—Jehovah, the Father, became the Saviour of mankind.

This truth we would as strongly as possible impress upon all our minds. We endeavoured to point out last evening the doctrine of the Old Testament to be that Jehovah Himself would become a Saviour; and we pointed out that the New Testament account of our Lord Jesus Christ was only the fulfilment of the promises that were given in the Old. It is astonishing to those who have not previously sought through the prophecies to ascertain the truth upon this great subject, how frequently the declaration is made in the Old Testament that Jehovah Himself would become the Saviour of mankind. Here, perhaps, we may be met sometimes by the reasoning of those who will say, because they attribute the ideas of the natural and unregenerate man to the doings of God, "But when man fell, how could God continue to love him, since he had departed from God's law, and rendered himself amenable to God's justice. Inasmuch as God is just, He must, as the moral Governor and Sovereign of the universe, inflict the pains and penalties of disobedience upon mankind?" But we sometimes make a mistake, a very serious mistake, in talking about justice. We speak of justice but we mean revenge. The man who has had a bond with a fellow-creature, and who finds that bond broken—broken, perhaps, through helplessness, or ignorance, or it may be through fault—who says, "I will have my pound of flesh; I will pursue through legal and all manner of means, every advantage I have"—he calls this often justice; but it is not justice, it is but revenge. The man who has had some insult offered to him, imagines that he must pay back in kind—he must give insult for insult, he must inflict blow for blow, and he calls this justice. It is not justice, it is only the infernal passion of revenge. Justice is the persevering regard for goodness and right; it seeks goodness and right sometimes by punishment; when it sees that punishment will do the criminal good, and preserve society from his dangerous crimes. It seeks goodness and right, at other times—when it sees that punishment is no longer required—by mercy gentleness, and kindness; by every effort to reclaim. It is the persevering regard for a good and noble end. That is true justice: and it rejoices whenever it can forego punishment, whenever it can put aside pain; it rejoices rather to reform than to punish in any way. This is justice. And God, when man fell from His law, was under no manner of obligation to descend Himself to inflict punishment and misery, but only still to seek the good of man. Sin punishes, sin pains, sin is the fountain of sorrow. All that is needed when a man sins is to leave him to himself; the sin itself will punish, and he will see the punishment to flow out of the crime itself. Man disobeyed God's admonition. It was in reality a merciful admonition that God gave, when He said—having made for man every blessing—" Of every tree of the garden thou mayest fully eat; but of the tree of the knowledge of good and evil, thou shalt not eat of it: for in the day that thou eatest thereof thou shalt surely die." Many of us are rather negligent in reading, and suppose when it is said the "tree of knowledge," it means a fig-tree, an apple-tree, or a plum-tree; but "knowledge" does not grow on such trees. The "tree of knowledge" is a symbol of man's own knowledge, his own wit, his own conceits, when compared with the Divine wisdom and intelligence of the Most High. And when a man takes of this tree, instead of being taught to receive God's wisdom as the guide and the light of his life, he eats of his tree of knowledge. As he fell then, so he falls now.

But God guards him against it, cautions him against it—tells him in the day he eats of it, he will surely die; and he does die. That is to say, he does come into that state which the Scriptures call death; for it is very seldom the death in the Scriptures means the mere parting from man's body which we call death. The sacred Scriptures make very little of this death, because, in reality, man does not die when we say he dies. Man has two sides; he has his earthly side, which we all see, and he has his spiritual, his inner side, which men do not see with the earthly eye, but which angels see. And when we say a man is dead, they say "a child is born." When we say the outward house is broken, or is dissolved, they say he enters into a high, and joyous, and happy life; if he has, by the help of God, built up a heavenly state within. When the material covering of a good man perishes, the Christian mourners say, an angel is rising up to enjoy the higher beatitudes of an eternal world. He has risen a step higher than he was. He has risen; first, having lived on this lower stage of being, he has risen to a higher and nobler stage, more to live, not to die. "He that liveth, and believeth in me," says the Lord Jesus, "shall never die; believest thou this?"

It is not this death, then, that the Scriptures have in view when they are speaking about death, pains, and penalties. It is the death of what is holy, what is pure, what is happy and delightful in the soul. This is death; and the moment a man turns himself against the law and wisdom of God, that moment, by a necessity of his being, he dies. "In the day that thou eatest thereof, thou shalt surely die."

God's laws execute themselves; they are not like our imperfect laws. They require no constable to be sent to see that they are put into execution. God's laws are self-executive. There never was a happy man since the world began, who was a disobedient, a selfish man. In the day he acts against the laws of God, he dies.

But God is not only infinitely good, and pure, and infinitely merciful; He is holy. His mercy CANNOT bless the guilty, the impenitent wretch. It is not for want of God's mercy that he is not blessed. God's mercy, and God's justice and salvation always go together. In reading the sacred volume this is a remark worthy of notice. It is not, as we often think, when we are under the influence of the state of mind of which the Psalmist speaks in the 50th Psalm, "Thou thoughtest that I was altogether such an one as thyself." When we think of God's justice, we, as I before said, often fancy that revenge is justice. We think of punishment, of His infliction of terrible torments. But it is not so represented in the sacred Scriptures. You will find justice and salvation go together there. He says, "Look unto me, and be ye saved, all the ends of the earth; for I am God, and there is none else"—"a just God and a Saviour; there is none beside me." And when the Lord Jesus was announced to come into the world, it is said, "He is just, and having salvation." He was executing God's justice, because God's justice means the persevering Divine energy that seeks to bless by reconciling man to Himself—bringing him back again to right and to order. This is what God's justice causes Him to do. "He is just, and having salvation," and therefore it is that the sacred Scriptures present the same glorious God that made the world, as in the person of Jesus Christ, coming to save the world. Look at John i. 10-12,—"He was in the world, and the world was made by Him, and the world knew Him not. He came unto His own, and His own received Him not. But as many as received Him, to them gave He power to become the sons of God." It was, therefore, the one glorious Jehovah Himself who promised, in a vast number of passages in the Old Testament, that He would become a Saviour; that He would come to redeem from hell and sin; it was this glorious personage who did come, and enabled the good upon earth to say, in the language of Zacharias, in the 1st of Luke, and at the 68th verse, "Blessed be the Lord God of Israel, for He hath visited and redeemed His people."

Never forget, then, this grand element in considering the true doctrine of the Atonement—that it was the God of love Himself, under the name of Jesus Christ, that came to save His people from their sins.

"But," it will be asked, "What did He come to save them from—if God was not angry, and going to destroy mankind, from what did He come to save them?" First, and this is the first part of the doctrine of the Atonement, He came to save mankind from the power of HELL. There is a law of spiritual affinity. For there are spiritual laws that affect minds in a similar way to the natural laws that affect matter. And as, by a law of natural affinity, like bodies come together and form themselves into appropriate masses, so by a law of spiritual affinity like minds come together and form themselves into close connection. This has been expressed in rude language sometimes by the old proverb, "Birds of a feather flock together." We see it is so in the gatherings that take place amongst men. But the Scriptures open up the truth, and experience confirms the same series of facts, that evil men and evil spirits become connected together. Hence, it is stated in the Scriptures that "Whosoever committeth sin is the servant of sin" —that wicked spirits associate with wicked men; so that if a person, first of all, endeavours to pay some attention to religion, and cast the evil spirit out of himself, but after a time begins to go back to his folly again, to wallow in iniquity, "Then goeth he and taketh with him seven other spirits more wicked than himself, and they enter in and dwell there; and the last state of that man is worse than the first." Experience confirms this.

Every one knows that in a bad man there is constantly a series of suggestions being made, leading him to be worse; he never shows himself as bad as he feels. There is a stirring from within impelling him to profounder depths of folly and sin. He restrains himself to a great extent to make a decent appearance before men, but there is always a pressure to a deeper gulf of evil, which keeps him pressing on downwards and forwards; there is a something worse than himself dragging him lower and lower. Just so, on the other hand, a good man finds something better and better still, leading him higher and higher, because good men on earth and good angels of heaven are united together. He that loves the holy precepts of the Almighty, finds himself in that sort of company of which St. Paul speaks when he says, "Ye are come unto Mount Sion, and the city of the living God, the heavenly Jerusalem, and to an innumerable company of angels, to the general assembly and church of the firstborn, which are written in heaven, and to God the judge of all, and to the spirits of just men made perfect." It is these holy ones that are associated with him of whom Jacob saw the representation in the dream, describing the grades of being under the form of a ladder, and the angels of God ascending and descending upon the ladder. The ascending is a representation of ever aspiring to higher and holier Christian virtues; the good rise, and angels help them upwards; and when they have received the inward blessings of the Almighty, they then descend to bring them into life—they "go in and out and find pasture."

Now, from the operation of this universal law, which we cannot stay more particularly to amplify, but which is full of suggestions of the most practical and the noblest character, when men fell from God they associated themselves with wicked spirits. The more men died, and went into the eternal world in this state, the stronger did the influence of hell become; until at length it was impossible for any power but the power of God to break the yoke that was formed between infernal spirits and infernal men. Then, God Himself descended upon earth, first of all, to break down the power of hell, and to set men free. What said He when He opened the Divine Book in the synagogue?—"The Spirit of the Lord is upon me, because he hath anointed me to preach the Gospel to the poor; he hath sent me to heal the broken-hearted, to preach deliverance to the captive, the opening of the prisons to them which were bound; the recovering of sight to the blind, to set at liberty them that are bruised."—Luke iv. 18; Isa. lxi. 1.

The human race at that time had become inveigled by the power of darkness, until they were laid prostrate. Judaism in its fallen perverted condition—Gentilism in its myriad idolatries, everything awful and abominable threw its infernal influence over human souls, and no power but God's could break that influence. Hence you will find it said in Isaiah lix. 19,—" When the enemy shall come in like a flood, the Spirit of the Lord shall lift up a standard against him, and the Redeemer shall come to Zion."

This, then, was the first part of the grand work that had to be performed. The power of hell was to be vanquished, and our Heavenly Father was to do it, because He alone could do it. He, therefore, came to be our Saviour and Redeemer. In His life, you read His great work; in almost every chapter of the Gospel He was casting out devils. He was removing those terrible diseases that the devils inflicted upon men. He was saying, "Go out of him, thou unclean spirit," and His Divine word was triumphant. In death He was triumphing, as the Apostle says in Hebrews ii. 14,—and in many other places the same truth is stated,—"that through death he might destroy him that had the power of death, that is, the devil." In death, therefore, the Lord died for us as He had lived for us, and He rose again for us. This grand first operation of the Atonement was the destruction in life and in death of all the infernal power that oppressed the human race. By reason of His overcoming the powers of hell, mankind were then set free, and they have since kept free. You and I are free at this moment; no longer trodden down as men had been by the influence of a power they could not control. From that time to this, the victory of our Saviour has made every man free to choose his life, and what he will be; to walk onwards, if he chooses, in the path of the regenerate life, and be formed into an angel-man. But if he will not, and choose the opposite, he has always to remember that if he sins he sorrows, and there is no fault to be attributed to any other than himself.

This, then, was the first part of the grand operation of the Redeemer God, to set free, and to keep free, all mankind from the power of darkness.

The second was, that He who had assumed a human nature to bring Himself near to man, might glorify and perfect this nature, and raise it into closest union with Himself, and keep it so as to be a channel through which His Divine power might for ever act, to keep man free. He perfected His human nature. This is sometimes called "glorifying His Humanity." This was the second operation that was finished in and by the Saviour's death.

As we said before, we must never forget that the Saviour lived for us, the Saviour died for us, the Saviour rose again for us. Would, however, that no soul might depart from this subject without the conviction, that this was done not to satisfy any wrath or vindictive disposition, either in Himself or any other Divine person, but it was to satisfy His own love, to redeem man from hell and sin—to satisfy not wrath, but love. It was from love He came into the world—from love He lived for man—from love He died for man—from love He rose again for man—and from love He has been working in you and me to make us fit for Heaven and everlasting happiness in eternity.

This second part of the great work of reconciliation, namely, perfecting His humanity, is oftentimes stated in the sacred Scriptures. Take, for instance, Luke xiii. 32, "Behold, I cast out devils, and I do cures to-day and to-morrow, and the third day I shall be perfected." Not that His Divine nature needed any perfecting—that was perfect in itself, and always had been—but the human nature in which He became like His brethren, that needed perfecting. So again, when He had risen from the dead, and His disciples were mourning and sorrowing, they thought all their hopes were baffled. They were very like us, my brethren; they looked at things as the natural man looks at them; and they thought because Christ did not enter into their feelings, and make a kingdom in which they might be prime ministers and dignitaries, all was lost. They said, "We trusted that it had been He which should have redeemed Israel;" but when they saw Him crucified, they supposed everything had become blighted. But Christ said, "O fools, and slow of heart to believe all that the prophets have spoken. Ought not Christ to have suffered these things, and to enter His glory?" Christ entered into His glory through suffering and death; and there is no way of entering into glory for any of us, but by following His blessed footsteps, and suffering likewise. By dying to sin, and living to righteousness, He perfected His Human nature, going through all that His creatures have to go through—going through struggles in life and death; but He did it by His own power, because He was God as well as man, because He was the Father as well as the Son, and therefore He said, as you will read in John xvii. 19, "And for their sakes I sanctify myself, that they also might be sanctified through the truth."

The second part, therefore, was the sanctification of His human nature—the making of it perfect—glorious—in all respects, the fit body of His Divinity, and then raising it with Him to heaven. "For to this end," the Apostle Paul says in Romans xiv. 9, "Christ both died, and rose, and revived, that He might be Lord both of the dead and the living. He was Lord of the dead and the living from eternity as Jehovah, but His Humanity became "Lord of the dead and the living" when it was glorified and perfected, and made one in all respects with his inward Divinity; and He, from this humanity, poured out His Holy Spirit, because His Human nature formed a channel between the Divine and us. It was joining hands, as it were, between mankind and Divinity; it was the "mediator between God and man," and it thus forms the eternal link by which the power of the infinite God flows forth to purify evil men, and bring them into the likeness of Himself—reconciling them to Him.

The third part of the Atonement, is the absolute conquering, in each man, of his sins both of nature and practice, so far as man co-operates with Him; absolutely overcoming his evils, so that he is really reconciled to God. This is the third part—"Be ye reconciled to God." Christ has done His part. That was all perfectly done, completely done; but when that was done, then came the part in which man had to co-operate with Him. "Thou shalt call His name Jesus, for He shall save His people from their sins." The third part of the grand work of salvation is absolute deliverance from sin. "Behold the Lamb of God, that taketh away the sins of the world."

Now this is a part that I would especially urge upon the attention of all of us; for there is often a great mistake made upon this point. It is supposed by some that we are saved by believing only what God has done for us; and when they are told that this is not so, sometimes they think we do not believe that God has done this for us. But what we mean to say is, that God always does His part perfectly and completely—that is always sure to be well done, rightly done, unmistakably done, and done so that it cannot possibly be mended. But God has formed us free agents; He has given us the power to co-operate with Himself, so that we shall not be made happy slaves, but happy freemen. In fact, slaves cannot be happy, even with golden chains on. It is quite impossible. Happiness is the blessedness that comes from man's freely adopting the principles that make him happy. There is a great difference between pleasure and happiness. A sensual man may be pleased for a little time; a mere savage can be pleased with a feather, and tickled with a straw; and very much of what the world calls happiness is little better than this. The pleasures of eating and drinking, and of sensuality, gross or refined, none of these are happiness. They are pleasures. They may be voluptuousness, but they are short-lived, and gross and impure; they are often the gilded cup that contains a deadly poison. God intends us to be pleased, but He intends us to be more than pleased—He intends us to be happy; and happiness comes from adopting God's principles within—from becoming like God. "Blessed is the man that walketh not in the counsel of the ungodly, nor standeth in the way of sinners, nor sitteth in the seat of the scornful." It is not in riches nor in rank, it is not in position nor in power, that happiness consists. It is in communion with God that a holy heart possesses happiness, "I come not to take your joys away from you," said the Redeemer, "but that my joy may be in you, and that your joy may be full." This is happiness. And to become happy, we must not only believe as a fact that God is, and that Christ came, and that Christ died for us—not only believe these historical facts, but we must so believe them as to take in the belief, not only in Christ's death, but in His life and His sayings; we must believe Him altogether, not partially believe Him—and believe Him so as to love and be what we believe. No faith but this is a saving faith—and this saving faith begins when, as we before said, we believe Christ in His speech, in His life, in His death—and if we do verily believe Him, we shall immediately begin to fight against the sin that He teaches us to be deadly. The belief of a large number of persons is nothing more than saying they believe. As soon as they really believe, they begin to fight against sin—to look out what sin there is in them. It is not enough for a man to say, "I am a great sinner," and to join the Church, and say, "We have left undone those things which we ought to have done; and we have done those things which we ought not to have done; and there is no health in us." Many, many lips say these weighty words, but have no real heart-felt belief in them. If another person meets such a confessor half an hour after, and tells him what may be the very truth, that he is a great sinner, for he has a vile temper, or is unjust, and thus he is a great sinner: if he is an insincere Christian, he will at once throw the charge back, and say, he is nothing of the sort, that he is as good as his accuser is, and perhaps a little better. That is not the way saving faith acts. Saving faith is an inward light, which shows a man that he is a sinner; and every man is a sinner, not only in nature, but in practice, before the Spirit of Christ is born in him, and begins to make him a new man. He who takes the light of heaven and holds it over his spirit will find, if he does not sin in being a bad-tempered man, he may sin in being a drunkard; or if he does not in this respect disgrace himself, his name, and his character, he may sin in overreaching others—and if he looks well, he will find that he has the terrible root of self-love in him—though in him it may be somewhat different from what it is in his neighbours. The sin of selfishness is the old serpent that deceiveth the whole world. Now, Christ, when His holy principles descend into the human spirit—just as He and upon the serpent's head—that is to say, subdued the power of hell, the great mass of selfishness,—He comes to give to each of His people the power to conquer selfishness, by might derived from Him: "Behold, I give you power," He says; "to tread upon serpents and scorpions, and upon all the power of the enemy; and nothing shall in any wise hurt you."

Now, this is the grand influence of true religion. It is a thing we oftentimes overlook, but our grand life-work is to overcome selfishness in ourselves; to make us like-minded with Jesus. His whole life was the manifestation of love and disinterestedness. He was the embodiment of this infinite desire to bless others. What brought Him down upon earth but this? Though infinitely rich, for our sakes He became poor. He chose not to live in majesty, but as a poor man—as the head, the God, the ruler of the good and the wise. He chose to suffer scorn and contumely, disdain, wounding, and death; a death far more terrible than aught that a mere human being could experience—for there was not only gathered around His cross all that men could inflict, but all that devils could inflict besides—and yet from that cross of suffering no word of vindictiveness, of reproach, or condemnation came; but, "Father, forgive them; they know not what they do!" It was to inaugurate in us, by His power and by His example, this grand effort of overcoming selfishness in us and in the world, and thus forming a community fit for Heaven; and it is only just so far that Christ's salvation becomes embodied in us, that we fight against selfishness, overcome it, and are saved. It is impossible that the selfish man can be happy; and because we have not understood this subject it is, that very often, the Christian profession has not effected its grand end. Men, under the name of being Christians, have often cherished as much selfishness as if they had no such name at all. So that it has often been the remark that "professors of religion are as selfish as other people are." So far as they are selfish, so far they are not possessors of religion.

This overcoming of selfishness is a great business. It is a difficult battle to fight. It is a work which can only be performed in conjunction with our Saviour, step by step; but, without our being reconciled to Him, it is not even begun. He has done His part, but we have not done ours. It is impossible to make a number of selfish spirits happy. If we do not conquer selfishness in our lives, if we continue selfish, we cannot be happy anywhere; we have not been happy before death, and we shall not be happy after death. But many say, "If I can but get into heaven at last—just get in—I shall be so happy." You won't, unless you get into a heavenly state before you go. An owl is not happy when it gets into the sunshine, although the dove rejoices in the beautiful light of heaven. And why? Because the owl's nature is contrary to the nature of light and beauty. And, it is just so with a selfish spirit. For what is selfishness? It is the desire to have everything for ourselves, and nothing for any one else. Suppose there are twelve selfish persons put together, and placed in a palace, with every enjoyment at their disposal, but each one is trying to get the whole for himself; every one has got eleven enemies constantly looking out to see how they can over-reach him. And how can persons so principled possibly be happy? On the other hand, let the Spirit of Christ rule—let a man be saved from his sin by fighting against his selfishness, and he will be happy any where. How often we forget, and think it is only believing in certain propositions that is the work of religion. It is so believing, that we conquer our selfishness, and if not so, our religion is a sham. "He that taketh not his cross, and followeth after me, is not worthy of me." "If any man will come after me, let him deny himself, and take up his cross, and follow me." Does any one say, "I can't do it; if I don't look after myself, who would look after me? In this world it is everybody for himself and God for us all." That is the very reason the world is such a miserable world. So many act upon this principle still, though in every age it has failed. Although the world has tried all sorts of schemes; has put bad men into grand palaces; they have been unhappy. The rich and the noble have tried all plans to make themselves happy; have built great houses; have had a large number of servants; yet some of these are amongst the most miserable of mankind. Though in ever so splendid mansions, if the spirit is not right, there will be no happiness. That is the reason why we have so much yet, of which to complain. One has thought and believed his creed to be the right one; another says that he is right; a third thinks that neither of their creeds is right, but his view is the one to make people happy. It is not believing in any creed or no creed that makes people happy; but to ACT upon this, which is the essence of all belief—the belief in Jesus Christ, when He says, "Thou shalt love the Lord thy God with all thy heart, and with all thy soul, and with all thy mind. This is the first and great commandment. And the second is like unto it, Thou shalt love thy neighbour as thyself. On these two commandments hang all the law and the prophets." He who believes these so as to embody them in himself, and subdue everything in himself that is contrary to them; he who believes, showing he believes by doing it; he that passes his days in the effort to form his soul into the image of Jesus Christ, by power from Jesus Christ; He is the manly worker who is completing the work of atonement—of being saved from his sins.

This is an actual salvation, and he finds it in being a better man, a kinder man, a juster man, and a happier man, every day that he lives. He cannot accomplish it at once. It is not a dream or a fancy, it is the work, it is the battle of life. It is the Christian campaign against whatever is against happiness and against heaven. It is the battle which each man must fight, and as he conquers in it, he will become a little heaven in himself. "The kingdom of heaven is not, Lo, here! or lo, there! but the kingdom of God is within you." There is the kingdom of

God, and it descends into man's soul in proportion as the spirit of Jesus conquers in him the spirit of selfishness in all its ramifications. As he advances, step by step, getting victory after victory over every passion, every temper, every thought—everything that tends to make unhappiness within, and unhappiness at home—he will know he is on the way to heaven, because heaven is in him. Many there are who have thought only fancifully about religion; who still say, "If I did but know that I should go to heaven, all would be right; I could bear anything then." Why, it is not a difficult thing to know that. You are sure to go to heaven when you die, if you get heaven in you while you live. It is not a difficult thing for you to tell. How do you act? "God is love; and he that dwelleth in love dwelleth in God, and God in him." How do you act? Are you peevish with your husband or your wife? Are you fretful or anxious, constantly craving that others should make you happy, instead of trying to make them happy? It is not likely you know anything about going to heaven; you have no heaven within you. You must at once commence the work of struggling against sin, not in name or in fancy, but sin in you. Look out what there is wrong in you. We are often very particular indeed, but too often direct attention to the wrong place. We are bent in finding sin out, and we find it out in everybody but ourselves. We complain that every one is wrong except number one. Yet real religion thinks but lightly of the faults of others, remembering that we can never really tell how faulty others are. What we take in them as wrong, may be intended to do us good; but whether they intend it or not, God will make it good for us if we are right. Joseph, when he was put into the pit, and made a slave of, did not know that that was the right way,—that God would make everything work together for his good; but it was so. And so it is with us. Let us look to the Lord, and see what He is, and what He says. Let us pray to Him to give us wisdom to believe

Him and agree with Him, and power to work His will out in us, and then we shall have a saving faith which will really save us from our sin—our selfishness; and as darkness goes out, light will come in; as misery is cast out, joy will descend; as selfishness is banished, the love of God will come down, "and in doing his commands, we shall know there is great reward." We shall know that we have passed from death to life, because we really love the brethren.

This is the completion of the great work of atonement. Each man is really reconciled to his Saviour. "Abide in me, and I in you." Christ only descends into us as we enter into the Spirit of Christ, by living faith, by real love, by earnest obedience to His commandments. "If any man love me," Jesus says, "he will keep my words." "I cannot keep the commandments," say many. Well, either you or the Saviour is wrong; which of the two is it, think you? "Well, I cannot keep the commandments, and do as other people do." Of course you cannot. "I cannot keep the commandments, and be in a great hurry to be rich." Possibly not. "I cannot keep the commandments, and get the fame and applause of every one." Perhaps not; but let Christ be true, and let our conceits pass away. That the world has been so unwilling to do this, is the reason why the world has made so little progress in being happy. We are never reconciled to Christ while we keep selfishness ruling within us. We keep the Spirit of Christ away from us. We are never reconciled to Christ while our minds continue the same as they used to be, although we sing and talk, and perhaps read and pray. We may often speak of the means of grace, but forget grace itself. These things are means of grace, but they are nothing but means. "The end of the commandment," as the Apostle says, "is charity, out of a pure heart, and of a good conscience, and of faith unfeigned,"—a real obedience to Christ. This is the "end," the other things are only the "means." The singing, the praying, attending the chapel, the being Sunday-school teachers, and all the various things in which piety indulges; these are all good, all essential as means, but they are only means; they are not the end. The "end" is the formation in the soul of a little heaven; it is the sending out of the soul those tempers that make it a little hell, and especially overcoming self-love, which is the great devil that reigns there. Let us; each of us; ask ourselves what there is in us that the Spirit of Christ requires to be rejected, driven out, renounced; and if a man cannot find out any fault, let him ask his next-door neighbour. If he cannot see anything wrong, let him ask his wife, she can see; let a woman ask her husband, he can tell her. The likelihood is that they will find that they have to bring themselves into the right, as the Lord Jesus teaches it, and insists upon it, and then they will find that His glorious Spirit will give them inward happiness. And although they may have the storms of life still to contend with; although they may have sometimes the earthquake which will shake the ground beneath them; although they may have trials and troubles; although they may have the tempest howling over them, and the sea beating around them; let them then say—

"We'll welcome the earthquake, the wind, and the storm,
For these to the Spirit of Jesus conform."

It is Jesus, the possessor of heaven and earth, that asks us to do this. Our experience tells us that happiness is found in no other way. We have many of us had to experience all the different shades of the business of life, and have not found happiness in anything. Let us follow Him; the great head and Captain of our salvation; and as He fought against and overcame hell for us, let us fight against and overcome sin from His power within ourselves. Then we shall grow up "first the blade, and then the ear, and then the full corn in the ear;" and God will give us the blessing of His Divine approbation.

When the young prodigal decided to go back to his father; the father; it is said, saw him, and ran out to meet him; and fell upon his neck and kissed him. It is just so with our Saviour-Father. When we rise up, and endeavour to go back from our sins to Him, He always comes forward to meet us, and He will kiss us, and give us His benediction, peace, and happiness. We shall find that there is no need of doubt that we are on the heavenly path. Heaven descends within us; blesses us in our undertaking; fills all our efforts with the joy of the Lord; and if we do not become rich, what matter—whether we do or not, depends upon whether the Saviour sees that it is good for us or not. There are good men rich men, as well as good men poor men; the grand business of life is to aim at being a good man—at being a heavenly, a wise man, and leaving the Lord to do the rest. "Seek ye first the kingdom of God, and His righteousness, and all these things shall be added unto you." We are as soldiers, ordered to keep guard in the outward wilderness for a time, to see that no robbers break in; and if the soldier does his duty—performs his work as his master gives him commission and power—then death will not be regarded as a sad shade, a dark cloud, a dismal land, but as God's permission to go home—as the great Captain's allowance to leave the battle-wilderness in which we have been keeping guard. We are to go into His glorious palace, where all is happy, both within and without; where the images of God will reflect His glory in themselves and around themselves; where every angel will find every other angel delighting to make him blessed, and where true happiness must be, because all are like himself, lovers of God, and lovers of each other, as well as, or better than himself, and consequently his happiness will be just multiplied by as many angels as there are in heaven. Whatever glory, whatever blessing, whatever gift the angels have, all desire to give that glory and excellency to the rest; and thus every angel has as many friends as there are in heaven, and he becomes as many times happier as these can make him. He is blessed within and blessed without. It is from the spirits of the angels and from the blessing of God, that heavenly happiness exists, and where such happiness is, there must be heaven, there must be bliss.

Let it be, then, our work to look up to the great Saviour as perfect in all his doings; to co-operate with Him; to let Him work in us, and as He saved the world, to save us, until we become like-minded with Him; and then welcome life in all its varied forms; welcome death, come when it will; welcome eternity. The herald that calls us thither will be the messenger of everlasting love. Let us adore the great Saviour, who shall meet us and bless us there—He who said, "Where I am, there shall my servants be."

A gentleman desired to be permitted to ask a question on the subject of the former lecture, but he did so for the sake of truth. Leave was given.

Q. We read in the Scriptures that He (Christ) "sat down on the right hand of the Majesty on high," which seems to imply a sense of place. How can He sit down at the right hand of another person unless there be that other person?

A. The question arises from overlooking what should always be borne in mind, namely, that the Scriptures continually use images of outward things to convey inward meanings. The hand of God does not mean the shape of a hand, the same as it does in relation to man—it signifies the power of God; and when Christ is said to have sat down on the right hand, or, as it is in some places, 1 Pet. iii. 22, in the right hand of the Majesty on high, it signifies that He took possession of the Omnipotence of God. The "right hand" means the omnipotent power of God, and when the human nature was perfected and glorified, thenceforward it became the centre from which all Divine power flowed forth. This is stated by the Lord Himself. "All power is given unto me in heaven and on earth."—Matt. xxviii. 18.

Q. Are we not led to consider the right hand as symbolical of two meanings—the one symbolical of power, and the other symbolical of distinction and regard, that is, giving up the superior place?

A. The first idea is perfectly Scriptural, the second is a mistake. The first idea you will find is constantly borne out in the Scriptures, "There shall thy hand lead me, and thy right hand shall hold me." No one supposes that Jehovah used the outward hand, but it is His power that does it. It is said that Christ had all power given unto Him when His Humanity was glorified. It was thus that He became the centre of all power and might, or, as He himself says, the Almighty.—Rev. i. 8. If our friend refers to John v. 37, he will read that no man hath "heard His voice at any time, nor seen His shape." How could a person sit at the right hand of that which had no shape?

Q. I do not mean to affirm that Christ was seated at the right hand of God in a bodily shape, but that such might have been.

A. You will see the moment you give up the idea of there being another body than that of the Lord Jesus Himself, you give up the argument.

Q. Does it not mean giving Christ a superior place, as in the case of a chairman at a meeting, he sits at the right hand of the lecturer?

A. You could not think He would be superior to the Father? All that it means is, when His humanity was glorified, all power flowed from the Father through the Divine Humanity, that He is "the head of all things;" "in whom dwells all the fulness of the Godhead bodily." We are told to come to Christ, and we shall find in Him all the Godhead. He is Father as to His inmost soul; He is the Son as to the Divine Humanity; and He is King of kings, and Lord of lords as to His whole Godhead.

Q. How do you distinguish between the relationship which Christ and God and that we hold to each other, when it is said, in John xvii. 21, "That they all may be one, as Thou, Father, art in me, and I in Thee;" "I in them, and Thou in me?"

A. The distinction is this—that God in all things is infinitely perfect. We, at the best, are finitely so. He is presenting there an image of union to His people, and the union that is held before them is the union of His Divine soul and His Divine Humanity. It is the most perfect union that can exist; "I in them and thou in me." A union between the Son and the Father is an infinite union. But when God had assumed and glorified His human nature, and made it one with Himself, then from Him flows the Spirit, the Holy Spirit, to all His creatures, uniting them to Him, but in an infinitely less perfect manner than the Father and Son are united together—united them to Him as man can be united to God. There is just the same difference between the union that God has, and the union that men have, as there is between the perfection that a Christian has, and the perfection that God has. He says, "Be ye perfect, even as your Father which is in heaven is perfect." Although we are to be perfect in our degree, that is infinitely less than the perfection of God in His degree. The union of man with God in Christ is a union good, excellent, and happy in itself, but infinitely less perfect than that between the Father and the Son. Unless we view it in that way, we shall scarcely have that beautiful idea that the Saviour presents, when He says, "I in them, and thou in me." So that we are united to the Father by Christ, and in no other way. Why, then, do not men look to the Lord Jesus and go to Him? Why strain after others, and seek to climb up some other way, only placing the Lord at the end of their prayers, instead of at the beginning.

Q. Now, sir, I want to know something more on the subject of to-night. You have said very little about Christ's blood-shedding. Now, I read that "Without shedding of blood there is no remission." Will you explain this?

A. Very willingly. First, it is literally true, that if the Lord Jesus had not died, the world would not have been redeemed; His Humanity would not have been glorified; death would not have conquered; and man's love would not have been won. "We love Him because He first loved us," and God commended HIS LOVE to us, in that while we were yet sinners Christ died for the ungodly.--Rom. v. 8. In relation to all these great works, then, "Without shedding of blood there is no remission." There is also a spiritual sense in which this text has an important meaning. The Lord said, long before He had shed His natural Blood at all, "Except ye eat my flesh and drink my blood there is no life in you. He that eateth my flesh and drinketh my blood, hath everlasting life. My flesh is meat indeed, and my blood is drink indeed." The Lord's Divine goodness and wisdom are His Divine flesh and blood, His goodness is the bread of life; His wisdom is the blood of the New Testament. Unless the Lord gave His wisdom to show us our sins, and to give us power to overcome them, they would never be put away. Without shedding of blood there is no remission. Sometimes our sins are said to be put away by the Word. "Now ye are clean by the word that I have spoken unto you." Sometimes by the Truth; "Sanctify them by the truth; thy Word is truth." Sometimes by water; "I will sprinkle clean water upon you, and you shall be clean from all your filthiness, and from all your idols will I cleanse you." And, at others, it is said we are cleansed by blood; "These are they who have come through much tribulation, and washed their robes and made them white by the blood of the Lamb." All these expressions, Word, Truth, Water, Blood, mean the wisdom of the Lord seen in different aspects; and without the shedding of this Divine blood, there is no remission. I hope our friend in offering his question is thinking of the remission or putting away of sin, and not thinking of pacifying the wrath of God by the blood. I hope he is not thinking of the verse of Watts:—

> Sweet were the drops of Jesu's blood
> That calmed His frowning face;
> Which, sprinkled o'er the burning throne,
> Have turned the wrath to grace,

This is a libel on our Heavenly Father, whose love redeemed us. The passage says not "Without shedding of blood there was no pacifying of the Father; but no remission of sin." The Lord's blood acts upon man to redeem and purify him, not upon **God, who** is already love itself and mercy itself. The Lord Himself says, "This is my blood of the New Testament, which is shed for many, for the remission of sin." It is always the same,—to cleanse us, and to remit our sins.

Q. But you have not explained to my satisfaction how the justice of the Father was satisfied. Man sinned, God must punish him. How could God forgive without His justice receiving an atonement. Either Christ, or us, or justice must die, and Christ died for us.

A. Will our friend tell me who satisfied Christ's justice. He was just, and the Holy Ghost was just, too. According to our friend's scheme the three Divine Persons are alike in mind. "None is afore or after other:" none is greater or less than another. If the Father's justice required some one to be put to death, why did not the Son's justice require the same, and why did not the justice of the Holy Ghost require a similar sacrifice? If the justice of two of the Divine Persons could do without any death to appease them, why not the justice of the first person be satisfied in the same way? In fact, true justice never requires death, but life; never destruction, but salvation. You say either justice, or us, or Christ must die. Now, man did die; for to be carnally minded is death, the Apostle said, Rom. viii. 6. The Lord came in His love to make him alive again. The death of the Lord was not to affect another Divine Person, for there is no other; but as our text says, "God was in Christ, reconciling the world unto Himself."

Q. What have you got to say about Christ's intercession? The Apostle says, He ever liveth to make intercession for us He pleads for us, sir, with His Father.

A. Yes; the Apostle says He intercedes for us, and he explains where and how It is the spirit of Christ in us that intercedes, by inspiring us to cry Abba, Father, suggesting our desires and prayers. You will find it especially alluded to in Romans, chapter eight: "Now if any man have not the Spirit of Christ, he is none of His."—Verse 9. "For as many as are led by the Spirit of God, they are the sons of God."—Verse 14. "For ye have not received the spirit of bondage again to fear; but ye have received the Spirit of adoption, whereby we cry, Abba, Father."—Verse 15. "Likewise the Spirit also helpeth our infirmities: for we know not what we should pray for as we ought: but the Spirit itself maketh intercession for us with groanings which cannot be uttered. And He that searcheth the hearts knoweth what is the mind of the Spirit, because He maketh intercession for the saints according to the will of God."—Verses 26 and 27. Thus you see the intercession the Apostle means is that secret inspiration of the Spirit of the Lord Jesus, helping our infirmities, and leading us to ask for those blessings which He waits to give. In any other sense of interceding what a strange view it gives of the Father. According to the old doctrine His justice was satisfied on the cross, man's whole debt was paid. Why, then, need Christ to intercede?

Q. Christ was made a sacrifice for us; He was our passover. What do you make of that?

A. A sacrifice is whatever is dedicated to God. The "sacrifices of God are a broken spirit: a broken and a contrite heart, O God, Thou wilt not despise."—Ps. li. 17. We are exhorted by the Apostle to present "our bodies a living sacrifice, holy, acceptable unto God, which is our reasonable service."—Rom. xii. 1. To be a sacrifice does not mean to be punished, but to be dedicated to God, and our Lord's Humanity became a whole burnt sacrifice because it was altogether offered up, dedicated and consecrated to do the Divine will, and this from the most burning love.

Q. How do you understand the passage, "We have an advocate with the Father, Jesus Christ the righteous"?

A. It ought to be rendered, we have a Comforter with the Father. The word is "paracleton," the same as that employed in the Gospel when the Holy Ghost is called the Comforter. The Lord's Humanity is the Comforter with the

Father, not to comfort Him, but to comfort us. He is the "new and living way" by which we approach to God, and God descends to us. If the Deity were still as He was before the incarnation, unknown and unapproachable, we should have had no comfort. But by the Humanity with the Father the comfort of God descends to us. Through Him we have redemption, through Him we have regeneration, and every blessing. He is the door, He is the Comforter. There is one God, and one Mediator between God and man—the Man Christ Jesus. The Humanity, the man, is the Mediator, the Comforter, because in Him dwells all the fulness of the Godhead bodily. And as we come to a man's soul by the medium of his body, so we come to God by the medium of His Humanity.

Q. Is not my guilt imputed to my Saviour, Sir, and His righteousness imputed to me? If it is not so, how am I to get to heaven? Is it not said, "The Lord hath laid on Him the iniquity of us all"?

A. The doctrines of imputed sin and imputed righteousness are essentially false, and unworthy of God. They are doctrines of deception and make-believes. God, who is Truth itself, cannot view anything different from what it really is. He cannot regard any one as guilty of a sin of which he is not guilty; nor impute to any one a righteousness which he has not done. Just and right is He. The idea that God imputed Adam's sin to all his unborn posterity that he might condemn all, and then His imputation of the whole to the Lord Jesus Christ, and punishing Him for it, and pretending that this was the doing of justice, is one of the most unjust conceptions imaginable. It is utterly contrary to the love of God, the truth of God, the order of God, in fact, to everything Godlike. It is written, "He that condemneth the righteous and he that justifieth the wicked, these both are an abomination unto the Lord." It is true, as the fifty-third of Isaiah states, "He was wounded for our transgressions, He was bruised for our iniquities: the chastisement of our peace was upon Him, and by His stripes we are healed."

because he went through a sorrowful life and death for us that is, on our account, for our sakes. The warrior who dies for his country, suffers for his country's good, but not because his country's crimes are imputed to him. The Lord laid on Him the iniquity of us all; that is, He took into His human nature the iniquity which is the inheritance of ours. Our proneness to evil He took from His mother, because He was to be "tempted in all points like as we are." He then met all our evils and overcame them all. He bare the sins of many, and removed them away. It is not said the Lord laid on Him the punishment of us all, but only the iniquity. Our nature has become iniquitous by hereditary defilement from father to son, and He took it in its most defiled condition, and met our evils there; conquered them, overcame the hells which were in connection with them, and sanctified His Humanity. But this was only done by the intensest suffering, which He endured from love for our sakes. It pleased the Lord to bruise Him, to put Him to grief, because this was the only way in which man could be saved. His infinite love would not spare Him a pang or a sorrow; but they were sorrows experienced by Himself in His Humanity, for man's salvation, NOT LAID UPON ANOTHER TO GRATIFY HIS WRATH. By the stripes His love endured we are healed. It pleases every good man to follow the Lord. To suffer also, to drink of the cup that He drank of; not for his own purification only, but for the good of others. Our friend asks if Christ's righteousness will not be imputed to him; I answer, only as much as is imparted to him. Let him receive the Lord's righteousness by doing His commandments, for he that doeth righteousness is righteous, as John says, and then heaven will be formed in him by regeneration, and he will go to heaven. All the righteousness he has will be imputed to him, and he who is righteous shall be righteous still, and he that is holy shall be holy still.

An old lady addressed the lecturer, and said,—I was very much pleased last evening, but this evening you have made it appear that our Saviour's work is not complete. You have given man something to do. But you know, Sir, man cannot keep God's law, and His law must be kept by some one, and so He kept it Himself.

A. Many who speak of God's law, do so without reflecting that God's law consists of those wise regulations which are essential to man's happiness. God's law is what God's wisdom has prescribed for man's good. God has ordained that man should eat that he may be strong; but does our friend imagine that if somebody else eats his dinner for man, it will do just as well? God's law ordains that man should walk and work that he may be useful and healthful; does our friend imagine that if a lazy person believed our Saviour walked and worked, it would do just as well for his health as if he did it himself? Righteousness is as necessary to the soul's health as walking is to that of the body, but no righteousness will do man's soul good if man himself does not perform it. Our Lord says, "Whoso shall break one of these least commandments, and teach men so, he shall be called least in the kingdom of heaven. And I say unto you, except your righteousness shall exceed the righteousness of the Scribes and Pharisees, ye shall in NO CASE enter into the kingdom of heaven."

Our friend seems distressed at the idea that the Lord's work should be represented as not completed until man is finally rejoicing in heaven. But we should remember that salvation consists of two parts—God's operation and man's co-operation. God's operation is always perfectly done; it is man's co-operation which is imperfect. Failure is there. The Lord Jesus did His part completely in redemption. He made every man free, and keeps every man free. He has the keys of heaven and of death. He opens and no man shuts; he shuts and no man opens. His work is perfect. But if man still is not to be governed by God's laws, he will still be miserable. The Lord struck off his fetters and opened his prison doors, but if man won't walk out, the Lord will not force him to do so. It is precisely illustrated by railway engineering. The engineers undertake to make an excellent road, satisfactory carriages, and proper stations. They do so, and the works are finished. But he would be a very simple person who expected to perform a journey by believing that the railway was completely finished and well done. If he would not go to the station, and take a ticket; if he would not get into the carriage, and persevere to the end of the journey, the best-made railway in the world would not serve his purpose. So with salvation. The Lord redeemed mankind, and opened, maintained a new and living way between His own adorable nature and fallen man. But we must use this way, or the Lord will say to us, as He said to the Jews, "How often would I have gathered thy children, as a hen gathereth her chickens under her wing, but YE WOULD NOT." He would, but we would not. He died, but we did not. "Ye are my friends, if ye DO whatsoever I command you." The circumstance which our respected friend names, that the Lord kept His law Himself, shows its perfect and indispensable character. If any one might have dispensed with keeping the Divine law surely the Most High might; but no, He kept it Himself, to show man there was and could be no exception. What is this law, which our friend thinks the Lord kept that man might not have to keep it? It is essentially TO DO JUSTLY, TO LOVE MERCY, AND TO WALK HUMBLY WITH GOD. But can any one dispense with this and be happy? Can the unjust go to heaven? Assuredly not. He who is unjust shall be unjust still, and he who is holy shall be holy still. Any society formed of unjust men could not possibly be happy. They would overreach each other, filch from each other, be intense enemies interiorly, however they might seem. Love is the fulfilling of the law, the Apostle says, and we may all take it for granted that no real salvation will be ours until we can say, like John said, "We know that we have passed from death to life, because we love the brethren."

Q. Do you think we obtain any merit by our good works?

A. Not in the least. We have no merit either in our faith or in our work. All merit belongs to the Lord. We soonest discover our demerits when we strive in all things to do the Lord's will. "And ye, when ye have DONE all that ye have been commanded, say, We are unprofitable servants."

Q. Do you find, sir, that this doctrine of the atonement is as practical in awakening love to God, and obedience to Christ from love, as the common doctrine?

A. Undoubtedly, far more powerful and far more practical. Let the friend who asks the question look around at what is called Christian society, and notice how little there is in reality of a life of practical love, justice, and self-denial. Let our million of paupers, our 20,000 criminals, our frauds and adulterations, our ill-will abounding, and our hundreds of thousands of drunkards answer. Are these fruits of the religion of Jesus? No. They are the fruits of that perversion of His Divine religion which says,

> Believe, and all your sin's forgiven;
> Only believe, and yours is heaven.

They are the fruits of that system which says you can be saved *at any time*, and from being as black as a fiend, become as pure as an angel in five minutes or one minute. This terrible delusion, setting at nought all God's laws and all the training of life, has deluged the land with poison, and multitudes run after the spiritual opium, which produces a fond delirium while it saps the spirit's health, and makes the nation and its religion a derision and a byeword. Let it, however, be proclaimed by faithful, loving men, themselves exemplifying their doctrine, "The Lord loves all His children, and has created and redeemed men that they may have power to become His spiritual sons and daughters, and be happy for ever." Let them declare without equivocation, there is no happiness possible except by obeying the truth. There is no neutral ground; heaven or hell is in every act. Keep the commandments from a spirit of love, and soon would a change be felt. The habits of life would become habits of order, of health, of gentleness, and of right. The operations of commerce and trade would be transfused by the spirit of rectitude, of openness, and of sincerity. Fraud would be repelled as a destructive serpent, and business would become a religious work of constant delight. This great nation, transparent with justice and faith, sending out her sons, the exemplifications of her fairness, kindness, intelligence, and usefulness, repudiating any intrigue or any advantage at the expense of others, would make the gigantic crimes of war impossible; men would be reconciled to God and to each other. While, however, we wait and work for these great changes, in which "Old things will pass away, and all things become new," we have one present duty. This duty is to fight against our own evils. We know them, we can never be happy but by their overthrow and expulsion. The Lord made us to be happy. He lived and died for us on earth to save us from unhappiness. His spirit is constantly with us, to enlighten and to strengthen us. Let us work out our salvation with fear and trembling at first, but soon to enter into states of love and joy. Soon shall we be able to say, "We JOY in God, through our Lord Jesus Christ, by whom WE HAVE RECEIVED THE ATONEMENT."—Rom. v. 11.

THE THIRD LECTURE.

ON THE CHRISTIAN LIFE.

"For this is the love of God, that we keep His commandments, and His commandments are not grievous."—1 John v. 3.

PRAYER BEFORE THE LECTURE.

O Lord Jesus Christ, in whom dwells all the fulness of the Godhead bodily, and who didst magnify the law and make it honourable, be with us to-night, and bless us while we meditate upon Thy commandments. We know that of ourselves we have nothing good, but we look to Thee to be inspired with light, and strengthened with love. Gird us, we beseech Thee, with holy firmness to walk in the way to heaven. Impart to us the spirit of self-sacrifice, make us to gain in humility, faith, and love; and whatever of good we have or do, O grant that from our inmost hearts we may ever confess that it is of Thy grace and mercy alone. These blessings we ask in Thy own holy name, Lord Jesus, and for Thy loving-kindness sake. Amen.

WE have endeavoured in the two previous lectures to point out, first, the grand and clear idea in which the whole Word of God combines that the Saviour is "God manifest in the flesh;" the first and the last of all that we can know or love of God, who alone can mould us into his own image and likeness. In the second lecture we endeavoured especially to point out that this one God had followed fallen man, and was in Christ reconciling man to Himself, uniting the broken link of communication between Himself and His creatures, and by enabling man to abide in Him, pouring into him a spirit by which all his sins could be overcome, and his whole mind transformed, so as to be lovingly obedient to the spirit and laws of the Gospel.

We have now, in carrying on the argument, to endeavour to show that all which God intended in making us as our Creator, all that God intended by delivering us as our Redeemer, is to be realized only in those who seek to live by power from this great Saviour Jesus Christ; who seek to live a truly Christian life, by keeping His commandments. "For this is the love of God, that we keep His commandments; and His commandments are not grievous."

We are anxious, first of all, to draw your attention to the fact, that all God's operations since the fall, all the Saviour's dealings are for the purpose of rescuing man from the dominion of sin. His object in Creation and Redemption is to form a happy, glorious, blissful Heaven out of the human race. It is impossible for man to be happy, except so far as he overcomes his sins and receives from God the principles that form happiness. It is a mistake which is too often entertained to suppose that happiness is an independent blessing, an effect without a cause. This error remains long, and exercises a most deleterious influence upon the human race. They conceive that happiness is a gift that can be imparted to a person all at once, irrespective of the principles that are within him; it is not considered that happiness is a fruit which only grows on one tree, the tree of goodness and wisdom derived from the Lord Jesus. Misery is not an independent thing inflicted by some one else, but it is a fruit that grows upon the tree of sin—take away the sin, and you take away the misery; leave the sin, and it is impossible for a man to be happy. It is astonishing to find men so often overlook that this is really the case: they act upon the idea as if happiness could be given in the same way as a concert of music can be given. For instance, how often do we hear the exclamations uttered, "Well, I hope, after all, I shall go to Heaven," "If I can only get into Heaven at last, I shall be all right." "I do not care for anything else if I can only secure my salvation at last." These persons being under the false impression we have mentioned, namely, the notion that happiness is to be got as a gift afforded and given to man from without, are in total opposition both to human experience, and to that Divine teaching which says, "The kingdom of God cometh not by outward observation: neither shall men say, Lo, here! or, lo, there! for behold, the kingdom of God is within you." This we know from experience is the fact. For we find persons—and this experience glares upon us in every condition of life—we find persons in all the circumstances of outward gratification, possessed of wealth, possessed of power, of rank and dignities, of high situations, possessed of magnificent houses and gardens, possessed of a large retinue of servants; but do these things make the selfish and the evil happy? Every one knows they do not. That the king who in his inmost soul is a corrupt and self-seeking despot, is amongst the most miserable of the human race; not half so happy as many of those lowly subjects who on the cottage chair at their own humble fireside, are of that character of which Jesus speaks when He says, "Blessed are the poor in spirit, for theirs is the kingdom of Heaven." The "poor in spirit" are not to be understood as those who are in the lowest condition of society only. It is possible for a man quite poor in pocket to be amongst the proudest of the human race, and as miserable as the most towering of the ambitious. It is possible for a person in the very highest rank of society to be humble and lowly—nay, the very highest Being of all is the lowliest of all. "Come unto me," said the Most High when amongst His creatures, "all ye that labour and are heavy laden, and I will give you rest. Take my yoke upon you and learn of me, for I am meek and lowly in heart, and ye shall find rest unto your souls." He, though infinitely rich, for our sakes became poor, in order that He might be the servant of all, and the minister of all. It is thus, then, the possession of a heart that is humble brings happiness—humble enough to prefer God's will to its own will, God's wisdom to its own conceits, godliness of life to wickedness of life,—that takes practically the glorious maxim of a celebrated writer, who said, "All religion has relation to life, and the life of religion is to do good." This is the man, be his rank high or low, be he the inhabitant of a palace or the tenant of a cottage—this is the man who will be the godlike man on earth, and will enter into God's happiness in Heaven. "This is the love of God, that we keep His commandments."

Allow me to direct your attention to this important word KEEP, for there are many who imagine that love is a sentiment only, who mistake feeling for principle, who suppose that they love where they have a strong sentiment of admiration. But this is not true love. The Apostle shows what he means by true love, in saying, "This is the love of God, that we keep His commandments." It is of the utmost importance that this be borne well in mind; for a person may sometimes love very deeply, and yet not have, at the same time, a sensation of delight in loving; while, on the other hand, a person may have a strong sentiment of admiration and yet have no real love. A person will think sometimes that he has a strong love for doing good to others, when he sits enjoying the sentimental feeling of, "How delightful it would be to see all the world happy! How delightful it would be for poverty to be completely banished! How very delightful it would be for the philanthropic feeling to be carried out, so that all the world might live in magnificent palaces, and enjoy everything that is comfortable and happy!" And he may suppose that because he glories and gloats over this feeling, that he has the love of God, and the love of his brother; while, in fact, he will not deny himself of a single indulgence; he will not deny himself even of a chance of overreaching his brother in a bargain; he will not deny himself of an unjust advantage over another: he will not, in fact, put himself to inconvenience in anything that requires a subjugation of his own selfish passions, either for the poor person in the next garret or neighbouring cellar; and he supposes, nevertheless, that he has the love of God. But oh, how mistaken is he! "For this is the love of God, that we keep His commandments." Never mind whether you feel very pleasant about it at the time or not; you most likely will not; for by nature we are now so perverted, that to do good is difficult at first, although we have the germ of all that is noble,—although God has taken care that "where sin abounded, grace doth much more abound,"—although God has taken care that in every child there should be the commencement of the kingdom of heaven. It is not the will of our Father in heaven that one of these little ones should perish. He, therefore, has taken care that there should be the germ at the commencement of life of every noble power and principle. Not a child is born but can be an angel or an archangel, if he obey the Saviour, and work out his "salvation with fear and trembling." But, nevertheless, there is also around these heavenly centres in the soul a mass of impurity, of tendencies to evil, of selfishness, of the love of the world, of the pride of life—of a thousand things that have to be overcome; and consequently the spirit of religion, when it comes to man, and opposes his own active worldly life, which has become vivid and energetic within him, will tell him that he is to take up his cross. The Lord Jesus said, "He that taketh not his cross and followeth after me, is not worthy of me." "If any man will come after me, let him deny himself and all his faculties, and take up his cross, and follow me." Now, this taking up the cross is not anything of an external character. It is nothing wonderful, ascetic, or out of the way. Sometimes, instead of paying attention to God's ways we make some devices of our own; instead of looking at the crosses that really exist, we make crosses—extraordinary crosses. That is not the way of the Word of God; it is that we "keep His commandments." You will find that salutary work is cross enough. To transform the spirit into a state of order, of harmony with God's commandments, is no easy task. Though there will be comfort enough, encouragement enough; though the Lord Jesus will help us—for without Him we can do nothing; though His angels will be brought into communion with us—"the angel of the Lord encampeth round about them that fear him,"—and they will afford us help and encouragement,—yet, nevertheless, for the selfish man to fight against his selfishness will be a cross; for the worldly man to fight against his worldliness will be a cross; for the sensualist to fight against his degraded appetites will be a cross; for the ill-tempered person to fight against bad temper will be a cross; and so on, through the whole catalogue of evil For let us bear in mind that, in Scripture, all these sins are real sins which have to be subdued. It is not shams that we have to bring before you. It is a real change from evil that must take place.

There are some people who talk in a strange style indeed. They say truly "that the Lord Jesus was our Saviour—that He lived for us, that He died for us, that He rose again for us." All that is most fully and divinely true; but they go no farther, and say, "He carried away my sins at that time; He removed them. I have nothing to do with them, only to believe that He did it." While they have the sin of selfishness, the sin of hating, the sin of cheating, and a thousand other sins, and yet—because their religion is not a real religion, but a fanciful one, they talk this kind of nonsense, and say they are quite delivered from their sins; while, if they cannot see their sins, everybody else can. It is not a deliverance of that kind that the Scriptures invite us to think about. It is really to believe that the Lord Jesus is a living Saviour; not only was eighteen hundred years ago, but is now a Christ in you, as the hope of glory; not Christ thousands of years ago, but Christ in you—a living Christ; He who ever liveth to give you power to conquer sin, to implant in you the spirit of virtue and every excellency, and to transform you to the image of Himself. This is the living Saviour, the Divine Jesus, that "saves His people from their sins." This, then, "is the love of God, that we keep His commandments."

"Well, but," some will say, "keep His commandments, that is a very hard task, indeed impossible; we shall never go to heaven if we are to go by keeping His commandments—we must go to heaven some other way." Allow me to assure you that you will never go to heaven any other way. If you cannot go to heaven with keeping the commandments, you will never get to heaven without. For, in the first place, what are the commandments of God? They are, in reality, the laws of happiness. We might go through each one, and every one can do it readily for himself; and then see how impossible it would be to form a heaven on any other principle than on that of keeping each one of the commandments. Let us take, for instance, the first—that we are to love the Lord our God, that very adorable Being who brought Israel out of their state of bondage, and who brings us out of the bondage of sin, whenever we are made really free. "If the Son shall make you free, ye shall be free indeed;" and there will be no freedom without. If we love this glorious God and Saviour, He forms the centre of our souls, the sun of our spirits; from Him come grace and glory. Under His gracious smile, it is as if we were in the sunlight splendour of a spiritual day—all is beautiful above, within, and around—we have received blessedness, light, and love from Him. Well, suppose that a man loves himself, and does not obey the commandments: he is the little god of his own idolatry; he is always seeking how he can make others subservient to him; however the wavering balance of things may shake, he endeavours to give it a movement in his own direction. Well, suppose that a number of persons are collected together, and this is the principle in each one of them, what must happen? Each seeking for homage and gain to himself. Every man of them has got as many enemies as there are persons, because each one is trying to take advantage of the other—trying to take from him, and not give to him. Place these persons how you like, they cannot be otherwise than full of envy and uncharitableness; and this is hell, not heaven. So if a person does not keep the commandment, "Thou shalt not steal"—does not keep it in thought as well as in work, even such a one cannot form part of heaven. How is it possible to form a heaven out of a number of people of that kind? Each one is trying to take from the other, each one steals the other's goods, or happiness, or ideas; or in some way takes from, and does not add to, the comfort of the others. Could you make a heaven of people of this kind? It would be hell wherever you put them. So that you see the commandments are the laws of happiness; they are the rules of spiritual health. God did not impose them to put a burden upon His creatures, but because they were necessary. They are just as necessary for the good health of the soul—and the good health of the soul is salvation—as sound rules are essential to the health of the body. The word "salvation" is simply the word health applied to the soul. *Salus* is the Latin word, it is health for the spirit—to be in a state of health and well-being, to be delivered from sin and all its tendencies, and to be initiated into heavenly excellencies and all their virtues. This is salvation. "What doth the Lord thy God require of thee," says the prophet, "but to do justly, and to love mercy, and to walk humbly with thy God?" The essence of every virtue is justice; that is the cardinal principle—justice to God, and justice to man.

We do not sometimes see the whole force of Divine teaching in the Word upon this subject, for in our English Testament, the word "justice" in the original language is nearly always translated "righteousness," and righteousness has come to mean in general conversation rather piety than justice. A person is said to be a righteous person who is very attentive to religious observances. These are good, they are highly important to be attended to; they are the means of religion, but not the end; justice is the end—coming into a state of religious regard to God; that is, living holily from love to God, because He constitutes the foundation of our every blessing—loving Him, therefore, with all the heart, and loving our fellow-creatures as His children, and because we love them being just to them, dedicating to them those powers and efforts which God has given to us for the purpose of making our fellow-creatures happy. This is justice; and if, wherever you read "righteousness" in the English Testament, you will read "justice," you will find then that a large portion of the Sacred Scriptures is given to teach us to be just. "Blessed are they which do hunger and thirst after justice, for they shall be filled." "Except your justice shall exceed the justice of the Scribes and Pharisees, ye shall in NO CASE enter into the kingdom of heaven;" mind, "in no case," no exception.

Now, it is this cardinal principle of justice that is the soul of all the commandments. "What doth the Lord God require of thee, but to do justly;" mind, not to think justly—not to sentimentalise about justice, but to do justly; and in doing justly, also "to love mercy"—have a tender regard to those who need your help as you need the help of others—"love mercy," endeavour to help the weak as Christ helps you—"love mercy," and then have no claim for merit, no glorification of yourself, but "walk humbly with your God." The more you receive from Him, the more a debtor are you to Him. What have we that we have not received? The more we receive, the more we owe. There is no rule, therefore, for a person, for a real Christian, for one that is animated by the love of God, that keeps God's commandments—there is no rule whatever for him to imagine that he has anything to claim of merit, that he has anything of self-righteousness to boast. If his righteousness is not from God, it is no righteousness at all; it is mere pretence. We are to do what He has commanded us, and when we have done it, feel that to the Lord Jesus Christ all the glory and the praise are due. But do it; because there is no preparation for heaven, there is no real possession of the love of God but by doing His commandments.

But, again. Let us notice some objections to this idea. "Keeping God's commandments," say some; "well, I do not think that that is the way to heaven—that was the way in the old law; that was what was given to the Jews." And so it was; and it was given to the Jews for the very same purpose. God's laws are always the same. If we need fresh help to be assisted to become Godly, that is, Godlike—that Old English word is oftener used than understood, but it signifies God-like—being in our degree like what God is in His infinite excellency; and this was always the will and the teaching of God, and in the Old Testament you will find, He says, His commandments "are not a vain thing for you, because it is your life."—Deut. xxii. 47. They are the essential qualifications for happiness. "Oh that there were such a heart in them," the Lord says in Deuteronomy v. 29—"that they would fear me, and keep all my commandments always, that it might be well with them and with their children for ever!" Talk of keeping the commandments not being intended by God, why He intended men should be happy. He must have intended that they should keep the commandments. It is not the keeping of the commandments that makes misery. It is not keeping them. It is not doing these holy laws that is the cause of all the mischief that occurs with ourselves and others. If there were no sin there would be no misery. God has not created a single faculty, from the crown of the head to the sole of the foot, but what tends to happiness; it is our tendency to sin that makes unhappiness; and to come out of it is to come out of sorrow. "Behold, I give you power," says the Lord Jesus, "to tread on serpents and scorpions, and over all the power of the enemy: and nothing shall by any means hurt you." We cannot keep the commandments, we never could, without power given from God; but with the power that is given, we feel we CAN keep them, and we MUST. "But," say some, "that is a terrible heavy burden." What does the Apostle say? "His commandments are not grievous." It is a heavy burden so long as you do not like it—but come into the love of keeping the commandments for God's sake, and for the sake of your fellow-creatures. Love this duty, because it is essential to happiness; because it is the only way to become an angel, and to prepare for heaven; and you will find the "burden" get lighter, and lighter, and lighter, until at length it is no burden at all; but you "shall run and not be weary, and shall walk and not faint." You will find soon it will be your delight to keep the commandments. That is what the Scriptures teach—"Blessed are they that keep his commandments"—not blessed shall they be, but "blessed are they that keep his commandments." They will be blessed now, and that will be the warranty for their being blessed hereafter.

Those who do not enter into this Christian life are oftentimes afflicted with the fear and the anxiety that they will not go to Heaven. They say they wish they knew. It is no difficult thing for us to tell, if we are honest to the Word and to the truth, while we observe our affections, thoughts, and acts. He will go to Heaven who opens his heart to let Heaven come to him—he will go to Heaven who is heavenly. "He that hath wrought us," the Apostle says, "for the selfsame thing is God, who also hath given unto us the earnest of the Spirit." He gives us the "earnest" now. Heaven grows in those who keep God's commandments from love; and they find that inward bliss spreads its holy balm around and within them, because their hearts are animated by love and goodness to others. God blesses them as they work this principle out, and they "work out their own salvation with fear and trembling." But as they grow in love, fear is cast away. You begin the work of religion with fear, but you do not finish with it. You begin with fear, but as you advance in holy excellencies, fear passes away and a child-like love and holy affection for God grows and grows until it takes possession of the whole man; and at the period when our work is finished, it is but putting off the outward covering of clay, and we find that we are at once in harmony with "the spirits of just men made perfect," and are happy by the principles which make them happy, by making them good.

"But again," it will be said, "did not Christ come to keep the law for us, and is not His righteousness imputed to us? You are forgetting the Gospel, you are talking about the law as it was under the Old Testament." Oh! no. The Gospel came not to make man less holy, but more so. The Gospel came not to say that man need be less attentive to his life than he was before, but more attentive. Christ came in order to convey to man power to conquer the sins that were passed over before, when God was not so close to man; when His power was not brought down so thoroughly as it was when He was manifest in His flesh. But when Christ came into the world He brought more power to fight against these evils that could not be overcome before, so that man could conquer his selfishness, could become Christ-like. And it is the great end of Christianity to make Christ's men. The word "Christian" means a Christ's man—one who is truly living because the Spirit of Christ lives in him. And although he cannot become entirely conformed to his Heavenly Master all at once, he can begin at once; and as he pursues the blessed course mentioned in our text—"This is the love of God, that we keep His commandments"—and prays to Jesus Christ from day to day for more power, for more faithful obedience, he will find that he goes on and on, conquering one class of evils after another as they are presented to him—just as the Israelites in going from Egypt to Canaan conquered one class of enemies and then another, while walking through their wilderness. While we are walking through our wilderness we shall have power given us to overcome the various evils that infest and assault us—

"And never sit we down and say
There's nothing left but sorrow;
We walk the wilderness to-day,
The promised land to-morrow."

When we are thus by Christ's influence made to be Christ's men and prepared for Heaven, the angelic character being formed becomes animated by love to Christ, and love to one another; and in such case our delight will be felt in doing good. Difficulties will be healthful exercises—everything will be joyous to us then. The homeliest comforts will be made delightful then; and when such men are congregated together in that glorious world where things are more plastic than here—that final inner world, the world of mind, where everything outside answers to the graces that are within; in such case, in heaven within and around, all things corresponding to the virtues of those that dwell there—there will be happiness from first to last. "Enter thou," said the Lord Jesus, concerning him who was faithful over a few things, "thou hast been faithful over a few things, I will make thee ruler over many things, enter thou into the joy of thy Lord."

But it may be said, "What are these works, these doings that you talk about so much?" Are they almsgiving, fasting, frequent worship? The answer is given in the text, "That we keep his commandments," in every work we have to do. It is an interesting view of the case to notice that the works of a person are the embodiment of what the man is. In every work that a man does, of course there must be some principle operating. He performs every work from some cause; and he who examines a little as to the origin of work, will see that a man does his works from his heart, from his will. He wills an act before he does it, and therefore the work is just of the same kind, of the same quality that his will is. And every work has this quality with it, that it confirms a person in the principle from which he acts. A selfish man by every selfish act he does increases that principle. Just, as is well known, a person who uses his hands very much in his trade enlarges his hands; so it is with every principle, the more we practice it, the more potent it becomes in us; and therefore he who would not have wickedness of any kind growing more deeply in him, must avoid doing it. "He that doeth righteousness is righteous," the Apostle says. "Not every one that saith unto me, Lord, Lord, shall enter into the kingdom of heaven; but he that DOETH the will of my Father which is in heaven," says the Lord Jesus.

A person advances in proportion to his faith in doing; and hence it is that the Apostle teaches, not only that the love of God is in keeping His commandments, but that faith also exists, consists, and is shown, in doing. He says, as you will find in James ii. 18, "Shew me thy faith without thy works, and I will shew thee my faith by my works." That is the only way that faith can be shown—by our works. For it is very clear that if a person has a knowledge of religion, but his works are irreligious, although he may have a faith as far as saying he believes this, that, or the other proposition or creed, he does not really believe it, he really believes what he does. If I believe that religion is better for me than irreligion, I shall do it. I may talk with another very largely about religion; say how much superior it is to be religious; I may pride myself on being very eloquent, and think I believe because I dream over it, and adorn it with imaginative pictures; but if the next day, when I come to the active duties of life, and I take the first opportunity I can of cheating the person with whom I have to do, it is evident that I believe in cheating, and I do not believe in truth and uprightness. If when a person is unable to gratify my wish I become angry and revengeful, it is evident I believe in anger and revenge. I may fancy that I believe in the excellency of the opposite, but what I really believe is what I do. And therefore it is that the word "faith" should always be remembered to mean, not a speculative, but a living active belief—a being FAITHFUL to principle, that is really faith. Both faithful to what Christ teaches, and to what Christ is—believing in His power and in His goodness—believing in His wisdom and what He commands us to do and be—that is faith; and he who really believes this, really acts from it. Therefore it is that the Apostle Paul says, in 1 Cor. xiii. 2, "Though I have all faith, so that I could remove mountains, and have not charity, I am nothing." That is, though I have all that speculative belief, all that idea about religion that would assert a belief in the whole creed, that is no use in the sight of God. Our real belief is the real inward disposition we have, that comes out in our acts, and is shown by what we do.

Well, then, it is very clear that the longer a person pursues the principles of heavenly goodness, through Christ, by power from Him, the more he becomes angel-minded, his inward virtues even give a beauty to his countenance and his entire appearance; they make him so that little children love him. Children see there is a something in him and around him that is delightful to them—that tends to make all who come near him happy, because the angel is becoming more and more formed within him; "This, therefore, is the love of God, that we keep His commandments."

Let persons, who become really religious, who believe in the end of their being, let them not dream about any fanciful taking away of their sins; but let them look into themselves, and see what sins they really have, and strive for their removal. Sins are different, the same as everything else is different. There is a variety in faces; there is a variety in virtues; there is a variety in sins. No two souls are alike, any more than two blades of grass are alike, and sometimes this is a cause of self-deception. A person that has no tendency to prodigality, but who is a covetous man, will pride himself upon not being so bad as his neighbour. He fancies that he is good because he is not of that outward, wasteful, wicked character that his drunken or prodigal neighbour is. The man who is voluptuous and drunken will frequently give himself credit for being a very superior man to another, who is parsimonious—and who will say, "God will rather have me than the skinflint that lives next door." And so each person justifies his particular sin by comparing himself with another, who may have some equally serious sin, but not the same as his.

Too many of us are content with a sort of lip confession, with no real self-examination. We say with the church, "We have erred and strayed from thy ways like lost sheep. We have left undone those things which we ought to have done; and we have done those things which we ought to have done, and there is no health in us;" but never look really within to see whether that is true or not. It is, no doubt, true. But we do not seek out our own particular sins, and see in what we so grievously offend. And very often it happens that you will hear of a person said to be "dreadfully religious, but terribly ill-tempered." Many are very strict in piety, but it is found they are very keen hands at a bargain. They are devoted to class meetings and church meetings, but are very inconsiderate about their shopmen; will drill them and exact unconscionable hours and labour from them, as though they were negro slaves. All these things are the result of persons using a lip confession, but no real confession, of evils being in themselves. They either do not look, or say not what they see. Yet that is the only way in which we can get the victory over our sins. It is not by general confession and a heedless life. It is a particular examination that is wanted, to detect in what we sin, and prayer to the Lord for power to overcome our sins when discovered. One may have a bad temper; another person may be naturally amiable, and have sins of sluggishness, sins of self-complacency, sins of being quite satisfied that they are all right, although they never make any earnest endeavour to use their talents for the good of their fellow-creatures, and can hardly be brought to see that they have any sins at all, because they see they are not so peevish as somebody else. But the conviction we should all have, is the conviction that we have many sins and many failings. Each has his peculiar plague, his sins of mind and heart, and he never can be happy until these are overcome by the active power and agency of the Lord Jesus Christ. Self is a terrible serpent, which, when once exposed, will be hated, and must be slain. It is a lurking serpent that coils itself up in some secret recess of the soul, ever ready to dart out and destroy. After a person has examined himself, and seen in what he falls short, he then reads the Word, and prays to God from day to day for strength, he will assuredly conquer. Read the Word so as to get the knowledge of God's truth; this is the "sword of the Spirit;" this is the power for overcoming sin. "Now ye are clean through the Word which I have spoken unto you," the Lord says.

It is by the Word we are saved from destruction; it is by the power of truth we overcome sin. And as we act earnestly, sincerely, patiently, diligently beginning in the morning, and going on through the day—beginning with prayer to the Lord, to give us power "that day" to be in communion with Him, and to act kindly and justly to all belonging to our home, and to all with whom we are connected in business—carrying this through the day into every act, sin will weaken in us, and heaven will strengthen. Some will say, "we shall never get on in the world if we do this," that is a sign you have not faith in the Saviour. The Saviour is He who made heaven and earth, and who rules it, but you have not faith in Him. You have a talking faith, perhaps, but you have not an actual living faith in the Saviour. The Saviour says, "If a man love me, he will keep my words;" "If ye love me, keep my commandments;" "If thou wilt enter into life, keep the commandments." Do you believe that? If you say you cannot get on without breaking the commandments, you do not believe it, therefore you have not faith.

Some people talk about going to heaven by faith alone, but if they have faith ALONE, they have not got faith. The virtues of religion do not exist alone. They exist altogether, or none of them are there. The trinity in religion is like the Trinity in God. The Trinity in God is in Him in whom dwells all the fulness of the Godhead bodily. The essentials of Deity are altogether in the One God. The trinity in religion is the same, the three great principles of love and faith and works go all together. A man that thinks he has love only, has not got love; he has only got fancy, sentiment. "This is the love of God, that we keep His commandments." "If a man love me, he will keep my words." "Love is the fulfilling of the law;" there is no love without that. He who says he has faith, and hopes to be saved by faith alone, he has not got faith; he is mistaken. If a person tells me that he wishes to go to a certain place, and he believes it is somewhere in a certain direction; and he wishes to go tnere as soon as possible. I tell him the exact way, but directly after I see he turns round, and walks in the opposite direction, I know he does not believe me. In all our other dealings with our fellow-men we judge their real belief, their real intentions by their actions. If a person tells me that he is a great friend of mine—if a neighbour that lives next door says that he wishes me well, that he is constantly thinking how he can promote the well-being and comfort of my family, but I find that he is doing all sorts of unpleasant things to make us uncomfortable, I see he does not believe what he professes. He professes well, but he does not mean it, and I do not believe his words. His actions tell me what he really means. And so it is in religion, in our relation to God; and therefore it is that the Scriptures set no value whatever upon a faith that professes to be faith alone. "Faith," says St. James, "is dead, being alone. The devils also believe and tremble." What better are they for that? And so it is with works. Works that are not from love and faith are not good works. If they are only appearances—virtues that seem to have a decent character, but do not really flow from love to God and faith in His principles—they are not good works. The Apostle Paul speaks of such when he says, "Though I give my goods to feed the poor, and though I give my body to be burned, and have not charity, it profiteth me nothing." It is quite possible for a person to do many kind things to a town—to give money to build a hospital—to give many gifts to the poor—to be very generous, and yet only to do these things as bribes to get the voice of the electors, or the sound of fame, or he has some selfish motive to be gratified in what he does. There is no goodness in that—these works are not good works, although they may look like good works; and hence the Lord Jesus said, "I know thy works," and He "gives to every man according as his works shall be." He alone knows what works really are, therefore it is that he who has got works without love and faith, he has not got good works; he has a name to live, but he is dead. The three virtues go together, and therefore St. Paul says, "Neither circumcision availeth anything nor uncircumcision, but faith which worketh by love"—all three together. Neither a person being very attentive to rituals and ceremonies, as the Jews were to circumcision and other rites; neither persons protesting very loudly against such things, as uncircumcision—neither of these are of any real value in the sight of God; it is "faith which worketh by love;" the faith that makes a man love the Saviour; the faith that makes a man love his fellow-creatures; the faith that makes him honest; the faith that makes him victorious over his evils; the faith that enables him to triumph over his daily failings, aiming to bring him more and more like his Heavenly Master. This is a saving faith, and there is no other.

Such, then, are the principles which constitute a Christian life; and they refer to the whole life, not simply to pious observances. They concern not simply the Sunday, but Monday, Tuesday, Wednesday, and every day in the week. They refer not simply to the closet, but to the breakfast and dinner table; the doings and dealings of the house in every respect. We have too long been in the habit of dividing religion from the world, and we have made a sour religion and a bad world. A person has imagined that by being religious on a Sunday, he may give himself many sinful indulgencies on other days in the week; and if he has been rather loose and easy in his business, he will make up for it by extra piety on the Sunday. All these are miserable delusions. Sunday is the spiritual market-day to lay in food for the rest of the week; but if you do not use the food, you will be no better for the supply. Sunday is the day for getting strength to help you to spend every other day aright; but if you do not use the strength, you will be no better for it. The Sabbath was made for man, not man for the Sabbath. Immortal beings were not made for no other end but to attend to the services of the Sabbath; but those services were made to help us to become men, to help us to obtain those virtues which compose the great character of a Christian. When men grow up more and more heavenly in all their being and habits, each Sabbath having more and more strength received from the Most High the Saviour, until at length they are quite ready to enter Heaven, and know and feel that they are ready, by the happiness they enjoy within, and the happiness that glows around them,—feel that they are ready to enter into the glorious world which is like their heaven within, where every act is filled with happiness, because every act is the outburst of wisdom and communion with the Lord,—then hath the Sabbath done its work.

Such, then, is the Christian life. Let us endeavour not to make any religion a substitute for this, but everything in religion a help to this, a channel to this. Let us not deceive ourselves. We are every day fitting ourselves either for heaven or for hell. Life is a serious thing, not a melancholy thing—but a serious, an important thing. This world is a training place for a higher and better. It is not a world that is of no consequence in relation to eternity—not a world in which we may live as we please, and at the last make a gasp and say we believe this and that, and hope God will take us and make us happy. If we trust to anything of this kind, we shall find it a broken reed that will fail us. As we said before, we must be formed to be happy; we must conquer our evils to be happy. There is no other way. Anything that seems of another character is an apparent exception, which, be assured, is no real exception. Let us bear in mind that Jesus said, "Except your righteousness shall exceed the righteousness of the Scribes and Pharisees, ye shall IN NO CASE enter into the kingdom of heaven." And why should we want to enter any other place? The life of religion is a thousand times better than anything else here. The life of sin never was a happy life. It is what we should endeavour to help our young people to see, that the life of religion, of true religion, of the religion of doing justly, loving mercy, and walking humbly with God, is the only way to peace and blessing.

I do not mean the life of religion as some people fancy it, is a happy one. This often seems to some to be the life of making themselves as miserable as they can—the life of going about and hanging their heads like a bulrush—the life of being as lackadaisical as possible. God did not make this beautiful world in which we live, in order that we might be perpetually spreading a miserable pall of mourning every day, and not being able to enjoy the mercies He has given us. "I came not to take your joys away from you, but that my joy might remain in you, and that your joy might be full." God wants to take away from us the things that make us miserable. He intends us to have all the blessedness that is in harmony with innocency; and only to fight against sins because they are contrary to the spirit of holiness and wisdom and happiness. At times it seems as if a man would be throwing away some advantage if he did not act unjustly. This is a mistake. He does nothing of the kind. If he would have all what is really necessary to his comfort and happiness in this world—and be prepared at the same time for everlasting happiness and comfort in the eternal world—let him live the life of religion—of real, living, practical justice and piety—This is the life of being as happy as our state of probation and preparation will admit, and we have heaven in addition. Why not live this life? Why not have continually impressed upon our children these blessed truths? Begin with the beginning of life, labour not vainly to the end. Too many talk of dying well; they should talk of living well; they are sure to die well if they live aright—

> Prepare to die? Prepare to live,
> We know not what is living;
> And let us for the world's good give,
> As God is ever giving.

> Give Action, Thought, Love, Wealth, and Time,
> To win the primal age again,
> Believe me 'tis a truth sublime,
> God's world is worthy better men.

Live according to the principles of the Lord Jesus Christ, and you will be safe in letting your dying take care of itself. "Be thou faithful unto death, and I will give thee a crown of life," says the Lord Jesus. "The kingdom of God is within you." Let these principles be practised in ourselves—be taught, by living them before our children—and let our children have the happiness of learning and understanding them, and being impressed by them; and oh, we shall save them from such crowds of sorrow—we shall preserve them from ten thousand afflictions, that rend hearts, that destroy the peace of homes, that make the world the battle-field, the Golgotha, of man, instead of being God's outer palace and training-place for heaven. We shall find, then, that this world is not the world of sorrow that too many have lamented to find it. It is a glorious world; it is a beautiful world. It only requires that men should be in their spirit like God, and this world would be like God's kingdom—showing God's happiness on an outer and lower sphere; but realizing what the angel sung, when John heard, "And the seventh angel sounded; and there were great voices in heaven, saying, The kingdoms of this world are become the kingdoms of our Lord and of His Christ; and He shall reign for ever and ever."

Let us hope that these truths may begin to permeate mankind. Let them make our little circles become gems, in which the beauty and blessedness of heaven will shine and be reflected on all around; and God will remember us in the day that He makes up His jewels.

DISCUSSION.

A GENTLEMAN said he very much approved of all that had been advanced, as to the excellence of a Christian life. No one could object to that; but what he did object to was making it an essential to salvation. He just wanted to hear what the lecturer had to say to that grand declaration of the Apostle, "Therefore we are justified by faith, without the deeds of the law."—Rom. iii. 28.

Dr. BAYLEY: First, I would remark that the Apostle does not say that we are justified by FAITH ALONE, without the deeds of the law. Faith has its part in the work of justifying the soul, but it has not the only part. The Apostle says in the preceding chapter, "For, not the hearers of the law are just before God, but the DOERS of the law shall be justified." Faith makes the intellect just by filling it with truth; love makes the heart just by filling it with goodness; and works make the life just by filling it with virtue. We are, therefore, justified by faith, we are justified by love, we are justified by works—but we are justified by none of them ALONE.

GENTLEMAN: But what do you make of that expression, "Without the deeds of the law"?

Dr. BAYLEY: It means without circumcision, sacrifices, ceremonies, or Jewish righteousness of any kind; for it was all either trifling in itself, or defiled with the idea of merit. To understand the Apostle's argument rightly, we must not forget the controversy which was then rife among the Christians, who were very many of them only imperfectly delivered from Jewish prejudices, and still thought they must keep the law as they had done, and add the Christian faith to the Jewish rites. In this controversy, keeping the law meant acting out the Jewish observances. You will find this illustrated in the Acts of the Apostles, chaps. xv. and xxi· particularly. In the 15th chapter, we are told, certain men which came down from Judæa taught the brethren, and said, "Except ye be circumcised after the manner of Moses, ye cannot be saved." When Paul and Barnabas had no small dissension and disputation with them, they determined that Paul and Barnabas, and certain others of them, should go up to Jerusalem unto the Apostles about this question, v. 1,

2. This subject was considered by the Apostles and elders, and "there arose up certain of the sect of the Pharisees which believed, saying, That it is needful to circumcise them, and to command them to keep the law of Moses," v. 5. Here it is most clear what is meant by keeping the law. It meant living as the Jews did, conforming to their ritual, being men of the letter of religion, not of its spirit. This is apparent in an equally striking manner in the 21st chapter. Paul came again to Jerusalem, and his coming once more produced great disturbance among the Judaising Christians. Some of the Apostles and elders evidently temporised very much. It was said to him, "Thou seest, brother, how many thousands of Jews there are which believe; and they are all ZEALOUS FOR THE LAW: and they are informed of thee, that thou teachest all the Jews which are among the Gentiles to forsake Moses, saying that they ought not to CIRCUMCISE THEIR CHILDREN, NEITHER TO WALK AFTER THE CUSTOMS. Do therefore this that we say to thee: We have four men which have a vow on them; take, and purify thyself with them, and be at charges with them, that they may shave their heads: and all may know that those things, whereof they were informed concerning thee, are nothing; but that thou thyself, also, WALKEST ORDERLY, AND KEEPEST THE LAW," v. 20, 21, 23, 24. Here, again, it is most evident that keeping the law had become a technical phrase for observing the Jewish customs, while faith meant a living belief in Christianity; a LIVING belief because grounded in love, and productive of just and holy works. The Apostle never meant to say that a man could be justified without doing God's will as well as believing it. No one speaks more strongly for Christian works than he. Look at the chapter going before that one from which our friend's passage is taken, where the Apostle says, God "will render to every man according to his deeds: to them who, by patience continue in WELL DOING, seek for glory, honour, and immortality, eternal life; but unto them that are contentious, and do not obey the truth, but obey unrighteousness, indignation, and wrath, tribulation and

anguish, upon every soul of man that DOETH EVIL, of the Jew first, and also of the Gentile; but glory, honour, and peace, to every man that WORKETH GOOD, to the Jew first, and also to the Gentile. For there is no respect of persons with God," chap. ii. 6-11. Nothing, surely, can be stronger than this; and it is the Apostle's constant doctrine. In the passage which the gentleman cited at first, the Apostle does not say we are to be justified by faith without any law at all, but by the LAW OF FAITH—that is, the law as the Christian understands it, in its spirit, and in living obedience to the Divine commandments. This was a righteousness before the Jewish law, and was always contained within its rituals and symbols. This is the RIGHTEOUSNESS OF FAITH. Hence the Apostle says, "Where is boasting then? It is excluded. By what law? of works? Nay: but by the law of faith," iii. 27. "Do we then make void the law through faith? God forbid: yea, we establish the law,"—v. 31. The law of the Divine commands, as the Apostle understood it, would be more perfectly done than it had ever been done before, for now it would be done "in spirit and in life." Hence he says again, "Circumcision is nothing, and uncircumcision is nothing, but the keeping of the commandments of God."—1 Cor. vii. 19. Again, "For in Jesus Christ neither circumcision availeth anything, nor uncircumcision, but faith, which worketh by love,"—Gal. v. 6. And once more, "For in Christ Jesus neither circumcision availeth anything nor uncircumcision, but a new creature." —Gal. vi. 15. Love, too, with the Apostle, is the ground of faith, and consists in the fulfilling of the law. "Owe no man," he says, "anything, but to love one another; for he that loveth another hath fulfilled the law. For this, thou shalt not commit adultery, thou shalt not kill, thou shalt not steal, thou shalt not bear false witness, thou shalt not covet, and if there be any other commandment, it is briefly comprehended in this saying, namely, Thou shalt love thy neighbour as thyself. Love worketh no ill to his neighbour, therefore love is the fulfilling of the law."—Rom. xiii. 8-10.

GENTLEMAN: You say, sir, that love is the root or ground of faith. Now, sir, it has always been represented to me the other way—that faith is the root of love. And if it were not so, would not the Apostles have told their converts to have love? But when the jailor at Philippi said, "What must I do to be saved?" the Apostle only said, "Believe on the Lord Jesus Christ, and thou shalt be saved."

DR. BAYLEY: It is very evident that the jailor was in the love to be saved, or he would not have asked the question so earnestly; and if to this love he added the real belief on the Lord Jesus Christ, he would be saved from sin and all its consequences. The love comes first, the belief second, and the practice last. If there be much love, there will be much belief and much practice. If there be little love, there will be little belief and little practice. "With the HEART a man believes unto righteousness, and with the mouth makes confession unto salvation."—Rom. x. 10.

GENTLEMAN: I have been taught that saving faith produces love and works as necessary consequences, as a tree produces fruit. Do you not believe it is so, sir?

DR. BAYLEY: That is a very common idea, but I fear there is much delusion hidden under its specious appearance. It would seem to imply that a person needs not concern himself about good works, but only about faith; since if his faith be of the right kind, that is, truly orthodox, his works are sure to be what they ought to be. Now, let us put this idea to a practical test. Are the works of professors of religion generally what they ought to be? Do the traders, the employers of labour, the labourers themselves, the clergy even, act upon the principles of the Christian faith? It must be answered that very few indeed do so—perhaps not one in a hundred thousand. Must we say, then, that not one in a hundred thousand has the right belief, or his practice would be perfect, since a true faith necessarily produces the right conduct? Nay, is there a single man whose conduct is in all respects right? Must we conclude, then, that not a single man on the earth has the right faith, or that there is some fallacy in this idea of a correct faith necessarily producing good works? Perhaps there are many fallacies in the proposition. We suspect there are. What is meant by a correct faith with those who use this argument? Generally it means a faith that the Lord Jesus died for us. But if it be asserted, that every one who believes that the Lord Jesus died for him will necessarily produce good works, we know it is not true. Great numbers who have this belief are very evil men, especially if they do not believe also that good works are necessary to salvation. Most Christians have the belief that Christ died for them; indeed, you will find very few who have it not; and yet the lives of most Christians do not abound in good works. The faith in the Lord's death if taken as the whole of faith, makes an incorrect faith, because it is incomplete,—it is a part of faith, yet only a small part; and it is wrong to assume the proposition that the Lord Jesus died for us as an entire faith. A true faith is a faith not in a single proposition, but in the Lord Jesus Christ; and a faith in the Lord Jesus is a belief in what He is and what He says. We never say we believe in a person, when we do not credit what he says. Now, those who do not believe that good works should be done as necessary to salvation, do not believe the Lord Jesus, who constantly teaches to do good works. "If thou wilt enter into life," He says," keep the commandments." "They that have DONE GOOD shall come forth to the resurrection of life, and they that have DONE EVIL to the resurrection of damnation."—John v. 29. "Not every one that saith unto me, Lord, Lord, shall enter the kingdom of heaven; but he that DOETH the will of my Father who is in heaven."—Matt. vii. 21. If we believe in the Lord Jesus as our Divine Saviour, and in the absolute necessity of a life according to His commandments, we shall be strongly disposed to do good works, but even then we shall do them voluntarily, not necessarily. The idea we are now considering seems to assume that when faith is received into the soul, its results as necessary offshoots, without will on man's part, will be virtuous works. We do not think

20. The faith which produces good works, must be a faith that good works ought to be done; a faith that the Lord requires them; a faith that heaven, where the Lord's will is done, can only be entered by those who have prepared themselves by doing the Lord's will here. This faith and life are procured not by necessity, but by constant effort. "Work out your own salvation," says the Apostle, "with fear and trembling."—Phil. ii. 12. If faith be regarded as a tree, we must remember that trees do not necessarily produce good fruit, but only according to their cultivation. He who grafts his trees with proper slips, and duly prunes the branches, digs, and enriches the soil, and in everything provides for their wants, will have an abundance of good fruits, but none others will. The process of being converted to a Christian life is shortly this: We first obtain the knowledge of heavenly things either through teachers, preachers, or otherwise from the Word; "faith comes by hearing." Having got the knowledge of faith in the memory, we are excited by some circumstance or other afforded to us by a merciful Providence to ponder upon it, and to be convinced of its necessity for us to save us from hell, and prepare us for heaven. The longer and more deeply we ponder upon it, and the more we read, reflect, and pray, the more does faith open its sublime lessons to the soul, and imbue the intellect. As we embrace the truth because it is true and good, we see it must purify our hearts and reform our lives, and we pray to the Lord that it may effect these saving works. At first we see but little of the light of faith; it is like a grain of mustard-seed, it detects our most glaring evils, and gives us power to reform them. Gradually its light increases, and we see more to correct, and we will to be more and more conformed to the Divine mind. Thus we go on by the power of the Saviour until every evil being subdued, and the life transformed, we obtain deep, interior, and lasting peace. All this proceeds by volition and effort, and no perfection comes of itself. The whole process is done by man, but by power from God.

GENTLEMAN: What are the good works that are to be done to work out salvation?

DR. BAYLEY: That is an important question; for too many have an idea that the good works of religion are only acts of piety, such as attending places of worship, reading the Bible, contributing to the spread of religion, and all such works as are connected with Sunday exercises. But this is a dangerous error. Works, are all the acts of life. Those of Sunday ought to be done, but those of the other days not to be left undone. The service of Sunday is really to enable us to do rightly on Monday and all the other days. On Sunday we ought to reflect, examine, and intend to improve in our whole daily life. If we do not use it for this purpose it is a fraud, an hypocrisy, and a delusion. Hear what the Lord says to the wicked worshippers of old: "When ye come before me, who hath required this at your hand, to tread my courts? Bring no more vain oblations; incense is an abomination unto me; the new moons and Sabbaths, the calling of asemblies, I cannot away with; it is iniquity, even the solemn meeting. And when ye spread forth your hands, I will hide mine eyes from you: when ye make many prayers I will not hear: your hands are full of blood. Wash you, make you clean; put away the evil of your doings from before mine eyes; cease to do evil, learn to do well; seek judgment, relieve the oppressed, judge the fatherless, plead for the widow."—Isa. i. 12, 13, 15, 16, 17. A person ought to pray, and to pray earnestly, for power to practice. But prayers are only words, and make a very slight impression when not followed by acts of justice and virtue. Actions flow from the heart; they form and reveal the man. Acts form habits, and evil habits enchain the soul. A man is what he habitually and freely does, not what he prays without doing. A person's real religion is just so much as appears in his daily acts in the form of justice and truth, just in deed and true in word. Every work is either good or evil. It is good if done from a spirit of religion; it is evil if done from a selfish, unjust, and impure spirit. The corrupt and fradulent practices which prevail everywhere reveal the real want of faith at the present time. Men have faith now in cunning, in fraud, in outward show, in fashion, in Mammon,—but little faith in goodness, in order, in truth, and in God. But a better time is coming. True faith is like a grain of mustard-seed now, but it will grow and spread and fill the whole earth. In the meantime, let me exhort my hearers, whatever their occupations may be, to do them from love to God and man, to execute them from principles true, honest, and just, and their every work will then be a good work, and their whole life be a life of religion.

GENTLEMAN: Is it your opinion, sir, that amusements are sinful?

DR. BAYLEY: Certainly not, if they are innocent, and take place at proper time. He who inspires the birds to sing, the flowers to bloom, and the sparkling spray to dance in the sunbeam, desires to see all His creation happy. To man, He says, "I come not to take your joy away from you, but that my joy may be in you, and that your joy may be full." Labour is now continued much too long. Shops are kept open with flaring lights, when both principals and assistants would be much better employed with cheerful and instructive books and studies, or healthy recreations. The worship of Mammon is a heavy, joyless curse; sad is it that men have not the courage to follow only the happy laws of their Saviour and Creator. Men destroy their health, and the health of their servants, in accumulating a mass of wealth which, from debilitated frames, they are unable to enjoy. They have been full of care, anxiety, and toil in getting it, and when they have realized the dream for which they have forfeited too often both conscience and health, find nothing but emptiness, weariness, and grief. If they had done business moderately and from just principles, business-life itself would have been a real pleasure; and when age rendered repose necessary, the man who had passed his life in virtuous, active usefulness could always look back upon it with pleasure, be an example and a counsellor to the young, and wait until his Lord summoned him to heaven.

GENTLEMAN: But we are told in the Bible, sir. that labour is a curse inflicted for the sin of Adam. It must surely, then, be right to avoid it as much as possible.

DR. BAYLEY: That is a popular delusion. Excessive labour is a curse, but orderly work is one of God's highest blessings. When Adam sinned, it was said, "In the sweat of thy brow shalt thou eat thy bread." But before that, when he was placed in Paradise, he was commanded "to dress and to keep it." Depend upon it, orderly work is the salt of life. Active labour brings forth everything valuable in life, and constitutes true dignity. The man who is sacrificing himself that his children may have nothing to do, is labouring not to bless them, but to give them a life of misery The Lord himself works for all: the angels are ministering spirits; and we must minister to the general happiness, too, by some useful occupation, or we cannot be happy. Wearisome is the life that has no useful aim—

"Triumph and Toil are twins; and aye
Joy suns the cloud of sorrow;
And 'tis the martrydom to-day
Brings victory to-morrow."

GENTLEMAN: May I ask, sir, what is the light in which the sacraments are held in the New Church? In these days we hear much of baptismal regeneration, when the sacrament is administered by a successor of the apostles; do you hold that doctrine, sir?

DR. BAYLEY: Certainly not. Regeneration with us is a fact, not a fancy. A man is born again when he receives from the Lord new tempers, new thoughts, and a new life. When as the Apostle says, "he puts off the old man with his deeds, and puts on the new man, which is renewed in knowledge after the image of Him that created him."

GENTLEMAN: But what has the baptism of a child to do with this?

DR. BAYLEY: Neither the baptism of a child nor of an adult effects this. It is only the outward sign of it. The water used in baptism corresponds to purifying truth; for that cleanses the soul as water purifies the body. Water is applied to the child or adult in baptism to signify that the inward water of the Holy Word must be applied to the spirit to render it clean from evils, both hereditary and actual. The Lord ordained this sign to be used for admission into His church, and no doubt when done from love to Him it has His especial blessing, and connects us more fully with the angels of His kingdom; and there is great propriety in the baptism of infants, because in reality the will of the Lord is, that they should in all things from earliest childhood be instructed in truth, and prepared for heaven. We baptize in the name of the Father, the Son, and of the Holy Spirit, because these are the three great essential principles in the Deity. The Father is the Divine love: the Son, is the incarnate wisdom: and the Holy Spirit is the Divine virtue flowing out from God. Man is inwardly baptized in the name of the Divine love as he becomes loving; in the name of the Divine wisdom or the Son, as he becomes wise; and in the name of the Divine outflowing virtue or operation, as he becomes virtuous in every act of life. This is what baptism signifies, and as our regeneration proceeds, this is what inward baptism actually is. It is worthy of observation that we read in the Acts of the Apostles, of their baptizing in the name of the Lord Jesus, xix. 5; a fact which teaches very strongly that they regarded that name as the name of the Father, and of the Son, and of the Holy Spirit.

GENTLEMAN: Will you favour us also with your view of the Holy Supper?

Dr. BAYLEY: As to the Holy Supper, the New Church teaches that it is the most Holy Sacrament, and the grand means by which the Lord most fully feeds the humble soul. The bread is the symbol of the heavenly bread of Divine Goodness, the Bread of Life; the wine is the symbol of Divine Wisdom, the new wine of the kingdom of heaven. When the natural elements are taken into the body, the spiritual food signified is taken into the soul, and thus the Lord sups with us and we with Him. This is the holiest act of worship, and the highest means of conjunction with heaven. We ought never to neglect the high and sacred privilege of meeting our blessed Lord, and being strengthened by His Divine Flesh and Blood. His Flesh is meat indeed, and His Blood is drink indeed. He who eats His Flesh and drinks His Blood has eternal life.

By prayer, by hearing and reading the Word, and by the Sacrament, we obtain Divine illumination, strength, and blessing, and by these all sins are subdued, and we rise daily to those graces which prepare the soul for peace and heaven.

GENTLEMAN: One question I should like finally to ask. I understand you to assert that a Christian life is in all cases indispensable for salvation. Now, I will not say but that is the safest course and the general way, but I have thought there were exceptions, extraordinary cases. Such, for instance, as the thief upon the cross. He had no time to live a good life, and yet Jesus said to him, "To-day thou shalt be with me in paradise." What do you say to that, and the eleventh-hour labourers?

DR. BAYLEY: We know nothing of the previous life of the malefactor, who said, "Lord, remember me when thou comest into thy kingdom." He may, for anything we know, have been a very good man in his ordinary life, and fallen into the fault for which he suffered from sudden temptation, like the Apostle Peter, who was undoubtedly a good man, but who, nevertheless, under severe and sudden temptation, cursed, and swore, and denied his Master. Moreover, an ordinary thief was not punished with death amongst the Jews, but made to restore, in some cases twofold, and in some fourfold. This man's fault was something different from what would imply an ordinary bad character. Dr. Kitto observes, "Some eminent writers are of opinion that he was, in all probability, not a thief who robbed for profit, but one of the insurgents who had taken up arms on a principle of resistance to the Roman oppression, and to what they thought an unlawful burden—the tribute money. They are of opinion, also, that it is far from certain that either his faith or repentance was the fruit of this particular season. He must have known something of the Saviour, otherwise he could not have said, 'He hath done nothing amiss.' He was convinced of our Lord's Messiahship, 'Lord, remember me when thou comest into thy kingdom.'" Kœcher tells us that it was a very ancient tradition that the thief was not converted at the cross, but was previously imbued with a knowledge of the Gospel. To all this I will add, the Lord who had previously laid down the law that "Not every one that saith Lord, Lord, shall enter into the kingdom of heaven, but he that DOETH the will of my Father who is in heaven," was the same Lord who admitted this man, and who knew him thoroughly. I don't believe He would break His own law, and therefore I conclude this man was a DOER of His will.

As to the eleventh-hour labourers, they had been waiting to be hired all the day, and when they were hired they obtained as much reward for their short time as the others had gained for all the day. They were placed first, for they denote the best principles of the soul, which come into operation the last. The whole vineyard represents the mind which has to be regenerated. The whole day is the whole of man's life. The different classes of labourers mean the different classes of affections which are made active in the soul. The first are the least excellent. As the lord of the vineyard goes out at successive times, he brings in fresh labourers, who have been waiting to be hired all the day, and at last those of the eleventh hour—so is it in our regeneration. The principles from which we first act in religion are low and selfish, much actuated by fear. Then we come into the love of knowing truth; then into the love of understanding the truth; then into the love of goodness, and of God, who is goodness itself. We begin with fear, but we come at length into that perfect love which casts out fear. The affections of this love are the eleventh-hour labourers. They are the last which shall be first.

And now, in concluding our subject for this evening, allow me to mention that only this doctrine of Christian life, which we have been urging, is in harmony with the great Scripture doctrine of judgment according to our works. If the doctrine of salvation by FAITH ALONE were right, all judgment of our works would be superfluous, since those who had the right faith would be saved, and those who had not would be condemned. Yet in NO CASE where judgment is referred to or described, is there any enquiry or declaration made in relation to faith. The judgment is always that of works. Let us suppose a case. A man has lived in villany and crime all his life. His career has been spotted with vice and selfishness, ever deepening, until he comes upon the verge of eternity. Then, terrified at the prospect, he recoils from the punishment before him, and he cries out with terror. Preachers come and tell him he must have faith that Christ died for him, and now, being powerless to act, and wishful to escape punishment, he cries out he believes, and dies. In the judgment, all his life will be declared, as it was, evil; and the law of judgment is, he that hath DONE EVIL shall come forth to condemnation. If the momentary faith will set aside the judgment of the life, undoubtedly judgment is utterly a vain thing, and the whole Word of God, which declares that we shall be judged according to our works, is vain. But it cannot be so. The very idea of this world is that of probation. Here we are men in the process of making, and what we make ourselves to be in actual life, such shall we be in the end. "He who is holy shall be holy still, and he who is unjust shall be unjust still." In the early portion of the Bible, we find it written, "if thou doest well shalt thou not be accepted, and if thou doest not well, sin lieth at thy door," Gen. iv. 7, and in the last chapter of the same holy record it is said, "And behold I come quickly, and my reward is with me, to give every man according as his work shall be."—Rev. xxii. 15. Oh may this great truth lead us daily to prepare, that in the spirit of justice and judgment, which is the spirit of heaven, all our works of every day may be done, and the sentence of our merciful Judge at the last may be, "Well done, ye good and faithful servants, enter ye into the joy of your Lord."

THE FOURTH LECTURE.

DEATH AND RESURRECTION.

"But as touching the resurrection of the dead, have ye not read that which was spoken unto you by God, saying, I am the God of Abraham, and the God of Isaac, and the God of Jacob? God is not the God of the dead, but of the living."—*Matt.* xxii. 31, 32.

PRAYER BEFORE THE LECTURE.

O Lord Jesus, God over all, blessed for ever, the Resurrection and the Life, grant us Thy presence, Thy light, and Thy blessing. We praise Thee that Thou hast formed us with immortal natures. We bless Thee for the gift of Thy Word, to train us for heaven. And we pray that Thou wilt so enlighten and strengthen us by Thy truth unfolded to-night, that we may indeed, in our daily lives, "seek first Thy kingdom, and its righteousness." Raise us, we beseech Thee, from the death of sin. Quicken in us affections of holiness and purity. Prepare us, by a holy life of love to Thee, and our neighbour; of faith in Thy wisdom and Thy promises; and of obedience to Thy blessed commandments, to walk before Thee in the land of the living. These mercies we ask in Thy own sacred name, Lord Jesus, and for Thy loving-kindness' sake. Amen.

It is impossible to conceive of a theme round which our affections more fondly group, or that is more interesting to us, than that which is comprised in the consideration of the termination of our career in this world, and our entrance into the final home in which all who are prepared become everlastingly happy.

The first remark to which we would desire to direct your attention upon this subject is, that death—meaning the termination of man's life here, and his entrance into a higher and an everlasting state of existence—is not, as has often been supposed, the consequence of sin, but is a result of the Divine laws from which creation has been effected, and of the Divine intention, which was, from earth, to people heaven. Man, as to his animal part, like all those myriads of animals which geology tells us lived and died before man was created, would also live and die. There is a death that has been the result of sin, but that is not the death of the body—it is the death of the soul, spiritual death. Any one who reflects upon the subject will easily discern that it is a mistake of the most decided character to suppose that the death of the body was a thing that supervened as a condemnation of man's disobedience, and had not been foreseen and intended by Infinite Wisdom. For if we remember and reflect upon the fact that the Divine admonition, when man was cautioned not to sin, was, "*In the day* that thou eatest thereof, thou shalt surely die," and bear in mind that what the Divine Wisdom declared must certainly have taken effect, will conclude that, as there was no death of the body on that day, it could not be that death which the Divine Being intended. Besides, if we reflect again, we shall see a reason to conclude that whatever inconvenience man received from the fall, Christ redeemed him from by His redemption; but inasmuch as Christ did not redeem us from the death of the body, that could not have been one of the penalties of the fall.

The death into which man fell by sin was not the body's death, but the death of the soul; that is, the death of purity, love, and light in the soul. The law from the first was as it is now—"The soul that sinneth, it shall die."—Ezek. xviii. 20. The death which paralyses all men's capacities for happiness is kept before us in the Word as the one thing to be feared. From this death the Lord, as the Redeemer in the Old Testament, ever strove to deliver us: and as the Saviour in the New, He brought life and immortality most fully to light. What was lost in Adam, was restored in Him. "He came that we might have life, and that we might have it more abundantly."—John x. 10. He died and rose again that we might live. The death induced by sin is conquered when, by the Saviour's power, we overcome the sin. Hence it will be surprising to one who has only thought of his body, and conceived of its rejection at last, as meant in the Scriptures by death, to read so often of death as being abolished in those who are saved. "Return unto thy rest, O my soul, for the Lord hath dealt bountifully with thee. For Thou hast delivered my soul from *death*, mine eyes from tears, and my feet from falling."—Ps. cxvi. 7, 8. "But, if the wicked will turn from all his sin that he hath committed, and keep all my statutes, and do that which is lawful and right, he shall surely live, he shall NOT DIE."—Ezek. xviii. 21. Again, When the wicked man turneth away from his wickedness that he hath committed, and doeth that which is lawful and right, he shall save his soul alive. Because he considereth and turneth away from all his transgressions that he hath committed, he shall surely live, he shall NOT DIE."—ver. 27, 28. "Make you a new heart and a right spirit, for *why will ye die*, O house of Israel ?"—v. 31. "For I have no pleasure in the death of him that dieth, saith the Lord God, wherefore turn yourselves, and LIVE YE."—v. 32. The victory over sin is with equal distinctness in the Gospel set forth as the victory over death "Even so must the Son of Man be lifted up, that whosoever believeth in Him might not perish, but have ETERNAL LIFE."—John iii. 15. "He that heareth my word, and believeth on Him that sent me, hath everlasting life, and shall not come into condemnation, but IS PASSED FROM DEATH TO LIFE."—chap. v. 24. "Verily, verily, I say unto you, the hour is coming, and NOW IS, when the dead shall hear the voice of the Son of God, and they that hear shall live."—v. 24, 25. "He that believeth in me hath everlasting life."—John vi. 47. "This is the bread which cometh down from heaven, that a man may eat thereof and NOT DIE. I am the Living Bread which came down from heaven; if any man eat of this bread, he shall LIVE FOR EVER."—v. 50, 51. "If a man keep my saying HE SHALL NEVER SEE DEATH."—chap. viii. 51. "Jesus said unto her, I am the resurrection and the life, he that believeth in me, though he were dead, YET SHALL HE LIVE; and whosoever liveth and believeth in me SHALL NEVER DIE."—chap. xi. 25, 26. "And you HATH HE QUICKENED, who were dead in trespasses and sins. Even when we were dead in sins, hath quickened us together with Christ; by grace ye are saved, and hath raised us up together, and made us sit together in heavenly places in Christ Jesus."—Eph. ii. 1, 5.

It may appear plausible to some that natural death was a consequence of man's disobedience, while they are ignorant that this death existed long before even the existence of man. But now it is well known to those that are at all acquainted with the condition of the earth, that geology teaches by ten thousand lessons, that millions of years before man stood upon this earth at all, both plants and animals lived and died—races even died out altogether. So that it would be the merest ignorance to assume that death —that is to say, the death which is simply the termination of one portion of our career and the commencement of another—that this is anything but an ordination of the Most High. The progression to a higher state involves the death of a former; and if sin—the only death that man need fear—if sin is shunned, then the death of the body is no curse, but is in all respects a blessing. In fact, to suppose that death—meaning earthly departure from this life— is other than a Divine ordination, is to forget that the earth is but the nursery in which God prepares His plants for paradise. This world is a world in which all things are covered up—all things have their probation. There is not a seed but what hath its sheath and covering. The seed gradually goes on to ripening, and, when ripened, it then throws off its covering, and comes out matured for its future use. It is in this light, therefore, that we ought to regard this world in relation to ourselves. Man is covered up here. This is not the man that we see; it is only the man's dwelling-place; it is only the bark of the man; it is but the outward covering. What we touch, what we have to do with in this world of nature, is but, as it were, the mask in which the real man lives until he is prepared either for future happiness or a future of self-will, and therefore misery; and when he is thus ripened for his future home, he leaves the body, and enters upon that home. If he has lived according to God's laws, he will then enter into all the fulness of God's blessings.

In this point of view, then, no one can suppose, with a show of anything like reason, that death is a thing which we ought to regard with terror and dread. Rather we should regard it as God's permission to move from this lower stage of being and to enter upon a higher, a holier, and a happier. It is the period when the soldier who has finished his campaign goes to receive the soldier's crown. The workman has done his work, and goes to receive his reward. In this point of view the Scriptures unceasingly present it to us. They bring life and immortality to light, and they present it in this aspect. Resurrection is immediately consequent upon death.

This is the first point. Resurrection is not a change that has to be waited for during thousands of years of sleep or dispersion; but resurrection immediately follows death.

In the second place, the Scriptures instruct us that man rises to his eternal home in a spiritual body fitted to that home; and,

Thirdly, that inasmuch as the earthly body is fitted for this world, and not fitted to a spiritual and eternal world, it is left behind, and will never be wanted again.

I. That resurrection is the resurrection of the man, and takes place immediately after death. The doctrine of the sacred Scriptures every one who is acquainted with the Holy Volume will know is very strikingly placed before us, both by special instances and doctrinal by teaching. As special instances, we may notice the Divine declaration to the thief upon the cross, "To-day shalt thou be with me in paradise." Here we are informed, not that this day a part of him would be in paradise, but "thou," the conscious being, the real man. "To-day shalt thou be with me in paradise."

There are some who take so strange a view of the body that they imagine the body to be half of the man, and that man is only half a man so long as he is without the material body, and will not be a real and full man until he gets it back again. That is not the doctrine of sound thought, nor of the Sacred Word. The Scriptures know nothing about man being a half man; they never describe man in the future life, or immediately after death, as having left anything of the man behind him. The thing is inconceivable in itself. Why should we imagine that man is a sort of nondescript after death? There have been a variety of notions upon this subject, but all confessedly mere conjecture. The Scriptures know nothing of them; sound philosophy knows nothing of an idea of this kind. For, as we have already said, the man is not the body; we feel that the man is something within the body; that, in fact, the body is only the mere instrument annexed to him while he remains in the world; and hence, science teaches us that no two hours from birth to death is the body precisely the same. There has been a change with you and with me since we entered this room. Every breath we exhale takes a part of the impurities of the used-up material of the blood, removes it, and breathes it into the room. Every inch of the skin of the whole body is moment after moment perspiring used-up material, and putting it away. So that every day a certain weight of the body is put off, which philosophy has taught us accurately to estimate. In the course of a very few years indeed, the whole mass of a former body is put away, and the new material that is taken in, in the way of food, has built up a new frame for us. So that we have had, in the course of seventy years, not only one body as was formerly thought, but probably ten or twelve bodies.

The closest resemblance to the constant change that is taking place in the material framework of a man—the house in which he lives—is that it is like a flowing water, ever flowing on, and ever having its place supplied by new material; or like, as the Apostle represents it, a tent that the Arab sets up in the wilderness for a short time. Our material body is a tent in which we remain for a period while we are trained for our everlasting home, and as soon as its object is accomplished, the tent is struck and removed. "For we know that if our earthly house of this tabernacle were dissolved," the Apostle says, in 2 Cor. v. 1, "we have a building of God"—there is something that will not be dissolved; we have another house. The earthly house is the earthly body; we have another house, the spiritual body, the form of the soul within, "a house not made with hands;" and this is not dissolved, but is "eternal in the heavens."

If, therefore, we have done without the first body we had, and yet the man exists, and grows stronger and nobler; if we have done without the second, the third, the fourth, the fifth, and sixth, it may be without a dozen, surely we may do without the last. A man, you perceive, is not the body but the soul, as Dr. Watts so beautifully sets it forth—it is the mind, it is the immortal part, it is that which does not change, it is that whose perfections are immeasurably more excellent than those of the body. This is the man, not the mere earthly form. The doctor puts this beautifully before us in the lines that have been so often written by us probably as schoolboys:—

'Were I as tall to reach the pole,
Or grasp the ocean in my span;
I must be measured by my soul,
The mind's the standard of the man."

It is this immortal mind, this glorious complex of faculties of a higher and nobler kind than aught of bodily excellence —it is this that forms the man; and therefore our Saviour said, not that thy soul or half of thee shall be with me in Paradise, but "thou"—because that is the man—"thou shalt be with me in Paradise." Precisely the same lesson is given when we are taught the parable of Dives and Lazarus; and it is said at the termination of the career of each they went to their final home. First, that "the beggar died, and was carried by the angels into Abraham's bosom." You see there is no notice taken of the material part. "The rich man also died, and was buried; and in hell he lifted up his eyes. The beggar died, and was carried,"—not half of him was carried, but the whole man was carried "by the angels into Abraham's bosom." As soon as his life terminated in this world below, immediately the angels were with him. Yes, and they were with him doubtless in his sorrows and in his trials, and in his triumphs too, while he remained in this world, though he could not see them. "The angel of the Lord encampeth round about them that fear Him." Those who come into the reception of heavenly things, come also into companionship with heavenly beings. We are the inhabitants of two worlds even now. "But ye are come unto mount Sion," says St. Paul to the Christians, as you will read in Hebrews xii. 22, "and unto the city of the living God, the heavenly Jerusalem;" and this is no vain, no empty declaration, but a real truth. If the eyes of our spiritual bodies were opened, we should now see the tenants of the heavenly world, as we see the inhabitants of the earthly world around us. We live in two worlds, though only conscious of one at a time; only distantly do we feel, because we are not prepared yet for the holy communications that might otherwise be had from these blessed beings; only distantly we feel, yet we do feel, what when reflected upon evidently confirms what the Sacred Scriptures teach. Who has not, in hours of discouragement, had some sweet balm of heavenly consolation, some holy thought dropt into the cup of bitterness, that has helped to stir him up to look for better things? Who has not had it suggested,—when cast down by the loss perhaps of some dear friend, some child or parent much beloved; when in utter mourning and distress, who has not had it suggested,—like the sweet tones of an angelic voice, "Not lost, but gone before; look up, think of what the Saviour said, and thus gather hope"? And have we not felt that the new star, which has passed from this hemisphere to shine in a brighter, is only an invitation for us to prepare soon to follow after? These infusions of heavenly light and comfort, these inward helps, that come sometimes when we are not looking for them, are all intimations that we are united to other minds than our own. Thoughts come from minds; they do not move about in the air. Good minds are joined, by God's providence, to better minds, and the angels of God ascend and descend upon the glorious ladder of Heaven. Bad minds unhappily are joined to worse minds, that gradually bring them down lower and lower. But we are in all cases, while we live here, the inhabitants of two worlds. We should never forget it, it is a truth of the highest importance, we are the inhabitants of two worlds. We have capabilities open to this outer home of our God, and others that open to an inner, a higher, and a holier home.

II. Well, then, when the man has matured himself, when he has determined his ruling love, when he has so fixed and formed himself that his time of probation can be ended, he has arrived at that period which all nature images,—for all nature is full of emblems of death and resurrection,—he has come to that period when just as the kernel is ripened, and the shell is broken, just as the caterpillar life is finished, and the butterfly comes out; just as when spring comes, and rises from the death of winter; just as when the sun that sets to this hemisphere rises to another, so it is with man. He leaves this world and its concerns, but to open immediately upon another and still higher world. Hence, as we have said, the instructions of the Sacred Scriptures teach us that the doctrine of the Bible is that the resurrection is immediate. Resurrection, say some, is the rising again of that which has died. But what does our Saviour say here in these words respecting the resurrection?—"And, as touching the dead, that they rise, have ye not read in the book of what Abraham, Isaac, and Jacob had undergone; that was the resurrection. "He is not the God of the dead, but the God of the living,"—it is the rising-up of the man. Hence the Apostle says, "For me to live is Christ, and to die is gain;" not loss—not the loss of one half of him, and that half the one which many people think is best worthy of their care: for a vast number in the world pay every attention to the body, but little or no attention to the soul. They think that the body is the best half, or act as if they thought so. But it is a most grievous mistake; it is always attended by misery, disadvantage, and distress. It is the giving of attention to the man's clothes, but murdering the man; and hence it is that the Apostle says, "For me to live is Christ, and to die is gain." And it is gain. The faculties of the soul are here, to a certain extent, cramped and trammelled, but there they will be free. Every one who reflects will see how very imperfectly he can carry out in his body the designs and purposes that he has in his soul. A person can think clearly, but he has difficulty in finding the words to express accurately what he means. A person can intend fully, but his body does not give him the powers to carry his intentions out. The soul is immeasurably more perfect than the body; and, hence, when we come into the soul-world, and when we throw off the outer casement of the body with its imperfections, we can see how fully it will be a "gain" to us. It will be a gain in increased power; a gain in increased perfection: a gain in the soul's living in a soul-world, in a mind-world, in a spirit-state of existence; and, therefore, whatever constitutes our living, interior energy will be at once carried out to represent it. The mind itself as well as all the materials around are adapted to represent and embody the purposes of the soul; and hence the state of things after death is as much more perfect than they are here, because man has thrown off the outer covering of the body, as the spirit is more perfect than matter. "For me," then, he says, "to die is gain." Our Lord himself expresses the same great truth when He says, "Thou hast been faithful over a few things, I will make thee ruler over many things: enter thou into the joy of thy Lord." All that we can be faithful over here, is comparatively a few things. We cannot make our bodies exactly what we would have them; we have great power and influence over our bodies, but that power is not only, by the heavy character of the material, cramped, it is also hindered much by the hereditary tendencies to disease and to imperfections, with which we are born, it is interfered with by the circumstances of our business, and where and how we live. So that it is not always the pure and noble mind that has a pure and noble and healthy body. Though there is a great tendency in a pure mind to make the body pure also, and there is a great degradation takes place in the body of a gross-minded, or of a bad and ignorant man. This has its limits; and we can only in a few things rule over this matter; but when we come into the eternal world, the spiritual body there, is the exact outbirth of the spirit—of the inclinations and principles that prevail in the mind. The good man is as beautiful as he is good. In the language of the Apostle, "God giveth it a body as it hath pleased Him, and to every seed his own body." We can see the evidence of that even in what we behold around us. Goodness, every one knows, has a tendency to make a person agreeable; even in his outward form, it throws a holy lustre out of the eyes, it gives a noble aspect to the face and forehead. Children like to be near a good man. A person who has been embodying in himself the Divine beauty of holy principles for year after year, acquires a heavenly aspect—and what is it? It is the beauty of the soul shining through the forms of the body; and when the forms of the body are removed, and you can see the soul itself, the inner beauty from which this celestial lustre comes, you can easily see then the meaning of the sacred words, "God giveth it a body as it hath pleased Him." But this is a spiritual body. It is remarkable that so many have overlooked the doctrine of the Sacred Scriptures respecting spiritual bodies—heavenly bodies; and have thought, everywhere when they have read of bodies, only of this outer covering of clay. But what

says the Apostle Paul? Read 1 Corinthians xv. 40, 41:
"There are also celestial bodies, and bodies terrestrial"—
that is, there are heavenly bodies, and there are earthly
bodies—"but the glory of the celestial is one, and the glory
of the terrestrial is another. There is one glory of the sun,
and another glory of the moon, and another glory of the
stars; for one star differeth from another star in glory. So
also is the resurrection of the dead. . . . It is sown a
natural body." This is the sowing place; on earth we are
sown: and here I would beg you to take a remark with you,
for sometimes we arrive at very imperfect thoughts of ourselves and of our destiny, from supposing that when we
come into existence at first that we are then men. God
makes us men at first, we suppose; but we should ever remember that when we are born into this world, we are only
born with the germs of manhood. This whole world is
God's manufactory for making men. This is the place, the
field where we are sown; and our whole career in this life—
all the activities of God's providence within and around us,
are Christ's operations, making us to be men, if we will
co-operate with Him. Simply to grow up out of bread and
cheese a certain height and weight does not make a man.
Very often it is but the imbruted serpent of selfishness
that a person is, who is yet the full height of a man. Very
often it is the embodiment only of the ambitious desire to
oppress others that we call a man: rather call such a one a
wolf. Very often it is but a two-legged brute that moves
about with vulpine cunning, and we call him a man. The
Saviour calls such a one a fox. God's characteristic of a
man is one that executes judgment and does the truth.
"Run to and fro," said God to Jeremiah, as you will read in
the fifth chapter and first verse, "through the streets of
Jerusalem, and see now, and know, and seek in the broad
places thereof, if we can find a man, if there be any that executeth judgment, and seeketh the truth." A person who is
too lazy or too sensual to bring out the noble faculties that
constitute manhood, and judge for himself—a person that

merely hangs on to somebody else's hook. is not a man. He only is a man who uses the glorious God-like capabilities of receiving and examining the truth. Coming into God's universe, and looking up and around, and seeing what God's truth teaches him, and examining it: this is to be a man. God says, "Come now, and let us reason together." He has given us the capacities of reason; He has given us the light and the understanding by which we can enter into the truth; and He says, "Come now, and let us reason together." He who does come—who comes to the light and endeavours to receive truth, and to see it in his own mind—not only because somebody else tells him it is so, but to acknowledge it because he beholds its beauty, its harmonies and duties: he is a man, who chooses truth, and says in the beautiful language of Cowper—

> And truth alone, where'er my lot is cast,
> In scenes of plenty or the shining waste,
> Shall be my chosen theme, my glory to the last.

This is a man.

Well, then, the sacred Scriptures teach us that it is man who goes into the eternal world. This man is the immortal being, and this man will receive the everlasting blessings of that world.

> "Angels are men in lighter bodies clad,
> And men are angels loaded for an hour."

The idea has prevailed with many that angels are a distinct race of beings from men; were made before them, and are altogether of a better class. But such is not the teaching of the sacred Scriptures. They teach us that angels are "men made perfect." They are always treated so in the volume of Heaven. When Manoah said to the angel that appeared to him, "Art thou the man that spakest unto the woman?" he said "I am." The first angels that are mentioned in the sacred Scriptures which appeared to Abraham, are called "three men." The angels that appeared to Lot are called "two men." The angel that spake to John said, when John was about to fall at his feet and worship him,

"See thou do it not: I am thy fellow-servant, and of thy brethren that have the testimony of Jesus: worship God." Nay, not only so, but when a glorious assemblage of angels was beheld in the eternal world itself, when ten thousand times ten thousand were seen by the eyes, the spiritual sight of John, an angel came and said to him, "What are these which are arrayed in white robes, and whence came they?" And John said, "Sir, thou knowest." And the angel then added, "These are they which came out of great tribulation, and have washed their robes and made them white in the blood of the Lamb." Evidently teaching that all the shining ranks which were then sending up the hallelujah of triumph to Him that sat upon the throne, were those who on earth had had their tribulation; had had their sufferings and sorrows; had had their persecutions and deaths; had made their robes white by the purifying influences of the Holy Spirit of Jesus Christ. "They have made their robes white in the blood of the Lamb." Hence, then, every one may see that just as those who have gone before us, those who have already had their trials and their triumphs, did not wait for some unknown period, when they should enter into the supernal beauty of "just men made perfect," but are already, with the palms of victory in their hands, clothed with the white robes of heavenly intelligence in all the glorious atmospheres of the blest, sending up their loving songs of holy praise and triumph. So will it be with us. When we lie down on a Christian's bed of death, it will be but to sleep for a moment, and then awaken in the Christian's glorious world of light and love. "Be thou faithful unto death, and I will give thee a crown of life."

III. But we have said further, that, as the result of this, the earthly body will not be wanted in the eternal world, and therefore will not be re-assumed. The notion that the body, the earthly carcase of man, is raised again after lying for a while in the grave, or having mingled with the elements, the gases that are in harmony with itself—that it is again to be brought up and form a part of man's everlasting body, is one that has been supposed to be taught in the sacred Scriptures, but is really not so taught. Like many other notions that have crept in, and been assumed as parts of Christian doctrine for a while, but afterwards the advance of intelligence or of science has shown them to be mistakes, it ought now to be rejected. The advance of science has shown that this is a doctrine that involves most serious and perplexing difficulties; and those who have still supposed that the Scriptures do teach the resurrection of the body, but who from science, have seen that it cannot be the truth, have been brought into very serious trial indeed. The way out, however, is precisely that which has been successful in relation to other points. It was supposed that the Scriptures taught that the earth was the centre of the universe, before Galileo so successfully controverted that notion; and the church of that time anathematized both him and all who taught this, and said it could not possibly be true, because, as they believed, the Word of God contradicted it. They found, however, that they must re-examine the Scriptures to see if they did really teach it; and it was found that the Scripture was right, but the interpretation was wrong. So it has been in a great variety of the lessons of the same kind. Now, it is just so in relation to this notion of the resurrection of the earthly body. Many a one who has been taught this from his youth, has supposed that he has only to take up the Bible, and open it, and he will be sure to find somewhere where it says that man's body is to rise again. But let me invite him to examine the Scriptures carefully on this point, and I can assure him that he cannot find a single text, from the first chapter in Genesis to the last in Revelation, that says either that the earthly body shall rise again, the material body shall rise again, the natural body shall rise again, this body that we have, shall rise again, or any words equal to these. The Scriptures teach that the man will rise—that the dead will rise, but never that the dead body will rise. On the contrary, they teach the very reverse. "In the mouth of two or three witnesses,"

It is said, "every word may be established." We give you the "two or three witnesses."

Take the ninth verse of the seventh chapter of Job, and you will read, "As the cloud is consumed and vanisheth away, so he that goeth down to the grave shall come up NO MORE." Now, what is it that goes down to the grave but the body? And that is to come up "no more."

Take, again, the apostolic teaching in 1 Corinthians xv. 35 and following verses: "But some man will say, How are the dead raised up?" Now that is the question. Some persons will say that when we speak of the dead rising, we mean the dead body rising; but this is plainly a mistake. We call men dead when they die to us; but there are two sides to them. When we say the man is dying, the angels say the man is rising. What is to us death, is to them life: what is to us a decease of being, is to them the commencement of higher being. Mortals say a man is dead, angels a child is born. So that, you perceive, this dying of a man is a mere appearance to us—it is not a reality. When we say that such a one died, the fact is, all that is meant is, he seemed to us to die—he departed this life; that is a far better expression than the other. He departed this life, but he rose to everlasting life; and hence, when the Apostle says, "How are the dead raised up, and with what body do they come?"—that is the real question, and you see how he treats it. He seems to treat it as being a very silly thing for a person to ask. He says, "Thou fool, that which thou sowest is not quickened except it die; and that which thou sowest, thou sowest NOT that body that shall be, but bare grain; but God giveth it a body as it hath pleased Him." That which thou sowest is NOT the body that shall be. That which is sown is a body of this world; it suits this world, it belongs to this world. This is the sowing place. Every boy who has sown a seed, knows that when he puts it into the earth it is not the same seed that he gets up again. The outer portion of the seed swells; it putrifies, it rots off, it mingles with the earth around, but from within the new plant rises. That is the image of the resurrection. The earthly body, which is suited to this world, is given to us; it is our first stage of life; but when it has done its work, it decays, it putrifies, it mingles with the elements around; but from within the man ascends. Just so the Apostle teaches—that there is one body for this world; there is another, the spiritual body, for the eternal world. "God giveth it a body as it hath pleased Him, and to every seed his own body." We must not be understood to mean that when our bodies are laid by, we get the other bodies for the first time when we go into the other life. It is not so. "Every seed has his own body." It is the body that is being formed within the outer body during our whole life, to which we have referred. An angel-minded man has a beautiful spirit; more and more beautiful as he perseveres in what is holy, pure, and good. It is his inner body that is meant. Only the pure get it in all its lustre and beauty. A bad man is gradually forming within himself an ugly spirit. The black-hearted man has a black and malignant-looking spirit; and hence it is that every one who has paid any attention to the great subject of how mind shows itself in matter, and has noticed, for instance, the low-minded criminals who are often brought up in our police-courts, will see such brutality and cunning, and malignancy of expression, in the very face, that he feels often he is near a dangerous person, and he would rather keep him a few yards off. It is the dark soul so impressing its ugliness upon the body; and when this is wrought out, so that the malignant desires of the heart have formed a spirit of vice, and have expressed themselves through the body, as far as the body would permit in this world, at death the mask is taken off; and then comes the time in which that is realised of which Moses spake when he said, "Be sure your sins will find you out."

Some people have wondered how judgment will take place, and have thought that it would be a strange thing for a person to come up before the bar of God, and to have his friends and neighbours and associates—perhaps his own family—to stand up there, and testify what he has done and what he has said, and so on. But that is not the way God's judgment takes place. We are preparing ourselves for judgment every day; writing our own characters ourselves every day. We are our own book-keepers in this matter. Every bad principle that a person deepens and strengthens, produces its expression upon his spirit; every foul, cunning malignity that a man cherishes and acts from, gives its expressions upon his own soul, and injures him before it does anybody else any harm. That is the book of life we are writing every day; either making it of the holy pages of life and love, or the defiled pages of malignancy and wickedness and falsehood, Oh, that I could impress this truth upon the mind and heart of every one before me! It is a fact we should never forget; no viciousness can we cherish, no wickedness can we love, without its doing its mischief within us. We know we cannot. Often that which we endeavour most secretly to do, is that which makes the strongest impression; and that which we have done without much concern and thought and contrivance has soon passed away. Those plans we have schemed about; that which we have proposed and contrived and cunningly carried out; that is indelibly fixed upon the soul. That is not blotted out, and never will be blotted out but in one way, that is by earnest, deep, practical repentance. Repentance is the only way in which a blotted page can be covered over. God says, in Ezekiel xviii. 27, "When the wicked man turneth away from his wickedness that he hath committed, and doeth that which is lawful and right, he shall save his soul alive." All his wickedness that he hath done shall not be mentioned in that day. The blotted book will be closed. His spirit will, in due time, have taken another and more beautiful form; and from the time when he honestly and in the sight of God repented and changed his mind and life, will he become new and purer and holier and more beautiful. Better had he begun earlier. The formation of the soul is not a mere mundane and transitory thing; it is the proper business of life. But when we do really change in heart and mind and life, immediately the change begins to take place upon the spirit; and, although we may have been filthy and impure before we begun, as we persevere, and work out our salvation with fear and trembling, we acquire a more holy and beautiful character. The vile body which we had before, gradually assumes the beauties which emulate the Lord's glorious body, "according to the working whereby He is able even to subdue all things unto Himself." This is the book of life, and when we go into the eternal world, we are what we made ourselves to be. God does not require any one to tell what we are, or to criminate us; we are there just what we have made ourselves to be: we stand in the light of eternity; what we have been doing, and have been in reality, there we are. A gardener, who truly understands the nature of plants, does not require in September to be told that such and such a plant has been neglected; he sees from the plant itself what has been going on; he sees from the effect what has been the culture. It is of no use to tell him that a plant has been properly placed, and trained according to true and proper means, and has had duty done to it, when it is a poor, miserable, wretched thing: he knows better. It is just so with God's plants. They need no foreign witnesses; they are themselves the books of their own lives; and the heavenly-minded have it written upon the ircountenances, upon their forms, upon everything about them. The Lord, the Divine Judge, and His angels see what they have been doing, and what they are. So with the infernally-minded; they have all their vices and impurities portrayed within them, and they, too, are there in the light of eternity what they have made themselves to be.

This, then, is the mode in which man enters into eternity. His spiritual body is his own body—"to every seed his own body." The heavenly seed is the heavenly body; the infernal is the ugly body. And so the Apostle goes on—"There is a natural body, and there is a spiritual body."

Not as some have supposed—there is a natural body, and there WILL BE a spiritual body; the natural body will be turned into a spiritual body: but there is a natural body, and there is a spiritual body. The natural body is the outward one, the spiritual body is the inward one; and therefore the Apostle goes on to say, in the fiftieth verse, "Flesh and blood cannot inherit the kingdom of God; neither doth corruption inherit incorruption." Flesh and blood cannot go there; it is a world for a different material. Flesh and blood going there would be something like a person attempting to put matter into thought, which is impossible—the two things are so entirely distinct. The spiritual world is only discernible and tangible to a spiritual body; the earthly world requires an earthly body. When a man enters into the spiritual world, he takes that with him which is accommodated to that world, and flesh and blood go to the elements to which they belong.

We have given, then, the "two or three witnesses," by which it is plainly taught that the material form is not required after death, and therefore we leave it for ever. It will never more be wanted by its present owner: it may go to form other bodies. On the other hand, as we have seen in the case of the angels, when they are described, they are not without bodies. All the multitude of angels which John saw, and which no man could number, of all nations, and kindreds, and people, and tongues, stood before the throne and before the Lamb," were "clothed with white robes, and palms in their hands." They must have had hands to hold the palms; and they must have had bodies, or how could they be clothed with robes? The beggar who died, and was carried by the angels into Abraham's bosom, and whose finger was mentioned that it might be dipped into water to cool the rich man's tongue, must have had a finger, or how could he dip it in the water? The rich man must have had eyes to have seen him afar off in Abraham's bosom, and he prayed that water might be given to cool his tongue; and if he had a tongue he had a mouth, and if he had a mouth, he had a head, and if he had a head, he had a whole body; and so the whole form is implied in all these cases—and, in fact, in every case in which the Scriptures give us a glimpse of the eternal world, they always do it so as to show that it is not a great way off: it is near to us. It is an inner world pervading this outer world: and as soon as a man's spiritual sight is opened, he sees that world. And when, therefore, the servant of Elisha was in consternation that his master was about to be taken away from him, the prophet prayed that his eyes might be opened, and he saw horses and chariots of fire. "Elijah was seen by Elisha when he went up by a whirlwind into heaven." The prophet's seeing implies the opening of his spiritual sight; and he beheld the world which is ordinarily unseen. The powers unseen, brethren, are, however, always more efficient—are always immeasurably more perfect than the things that are seen. The seer saw the world unseen—the glorious and everlasting world. And when we have our inward powers open to behold it, we shall see its perfections, its glories, just as John did. He was in the isle of Patmos when he was brought into the spirit, and then he saw all that he describes through the twenty-two chapters of his book. He was not wafted somewhere through the air, an immense distance beyond the stars, where some people dream that heaven is to be found—a region so far distant that, as some of those philosophers who have most profoundly gauged the depths of space tell us, there are certain stars so distant, that it would take millions of years for light from them to reach us! Heaven is not so far off as all that. But when John was in the isle of Patmos, and he was brought into the spirit, immediately he saw, he says, and he beheld his Lord and Master—he beheld heaven open: and so will it be with us. If our spiritual sight were opened by the Divine Being, we should also see what we may now know—that the two worlds are close together.

Well, then, all that is needed is that we should have a body adequate to that world when we pass from this; and such a body we have in the form of the soul itself. "There is a natural body, and there is a spiritual body."

There are a few places in the sacred Scriptures that have been supposed—some from incorrect translation, and some from other circumstances—to teach the resurrection of the material body; but when these are examined carefully, it will be found they all of them harmonise with the great lessons we have already traced, from the sacred volume. I have pointed out that Job taught that he "that goeth down to the grave shall come up no more." But others have supposed that they learn the contrary from what Job said in the nineteenth chapter of the same book—a passage that has been very much used because it was introduced into the Burial Service of the Church of England,—in which Job speaks of his body being destroyed by worms, and says, "yet in my flesh shall I see God." But if you examine the passage you will find that its strongest part is made up of italic words—words printed in a different character from the rest; and wherever you read these words in italic letters in the Bible, it means they do not occur in the original. They are what the translators supposed was meant, but they are not the words of Holy Writ themselves. In this passage you have "worms," and that is the first term that makes a person think concerning the grave, and what is done with the body in the grave; that word is in italics. The word "body" is in italics—the next term that has caused the passage to be thought of as having something to do with the body perishing in the grave. But, if the passage is read without these italics, you will find it simply expresses the confidence of Job, that though he may be brought into the extreme of sorrow and affliction; though his very reins might be consumed; he speaks of being so distressed by disease that he has scarcely anything left but his skin, "Yet," he says, "in my flesh shall I see God," meaning he would see Him before he died; and this hope was inspired into him—no doubt by God Himself, who intended to deliver him; and it was fulfilled—God did appear to Job. He was faithful, notwithstanding his affliction and bitterness and sorrow; and you will find at the end of his book it is said that God appeared to him, vindicated him, taught him that he had been quite right in following up his integrity and truth, and that his friends had been wrong in accusing him. It was no more reason when he was afflicted that we should conclude he was a sinner more than others, than that we should conclude our Divine Saviour was a sinner, because He was so much afflicted. All are sinners, and all need purification. God knows what we need, and how we need it best. But in Job's case, when God appeared to him, he referred to this very hope. In Job xlii. 5, it is said, "I have heard of Thee by the hearing of the ear, but now mine eye seeth Thee." In the former chapter he expressed a hope that his eye should see God before he died, and in his latter end it was fulfilled; he had seen God before he died: "So the Lord blessed the latter end of Job more than his beginning." So that when we take the whole teaching of this book of Job, it is entirely harmonious with the fact that man rises immediately after death.

Job himself again assures us several times that death is a final departure of man from the world and of the body to dust; neither will be recalled. "So man lieth down, and riseth not; till the heavens be no more; they shall NOT awake, NOR be raised out of their sleep"—Job xiv. 12. As the heavens will remain for ever, that which would not take place till the heavens be no more, will never take place. "Before I go whence I shall NOT RETURN, even to the land of darkness, and the shadow of death"—Job x. 21. "When a few years are come, then I shall go the way whence I shall not return"—Job xvi. 22.

There are two other passages of a figurative kind in the Old Testament which are supposed to teach the resurrection of the earthly body. But they are figures in the letter, only of the resurrection of the Jewish nation from political death and burial. We will notice them. It is written in Isaiah, "Thy dead men shall live, together with my dead body shall they rise. Awake and sing, ye that dwell in dust, for thy dew is as the dew of herbs, and the earth shall cast out the dead."—xxvi. 19. Again, in Daniel, "And many of them that sleep in the dust of the earth shall awake; some to everlasting life, and some to shame and everlasting contempt."—xii. 2. The key to these is given in the prophecy of Ezekiel, concerning the dry bones. The miserable state of Israel in captivity was represented by the valley full of dry bones. The restoration of their nation to their own land was symbolized by the resurrection and vivification of the bones, and their reconstruction into perfect bodies. Thus the Prophet explains it: "These bones are the whole house of Israel; behold they say, Our bones are dried, and our hope is lost; we are cut off for our parts. Therefore prophesy, and say unto them, Thus saith the Lord God, Behold, O my people, I will open your graves and cause you to come out of your graves, and bring you into the land of Israel."—xxxvii. 11, 12. They, then, who are said to be dead, and to sleep in the dust, are the people of Israel buried in captivity. Their being called to freedom, and raised to become a nation once more, and rejoice in their restored temple and the glories of home, is the awaking and singing of those who had dwelt in the dust. "Shake thyself from the dust, arise and sit down, O Jerusalem; loose thyself from the bonds of thy neck, O captive daughter of Zion."—Isa. lxii. 2.

In the spiritual sense, these texts imply the resurrection of religion in the soul, and of course have nothing to do with the raising again of dead bodies.

The New Testament also has a few passages which have in like manner been misunderstood, because applied to the body, when they ought to be applied to the soul.

The idea which should always be borne in mind when reading the New Testament is, that the soul of man in its fallen condition is dead, and the work of religion is to raise it to life and health. Its covering and pretences are compared to a grave in which the soul is entombed. It has to be brought out of these graves, and enabled to walk vigorously in the light of the spirit of the Saviour. With this view, every passage which has been deemed by the naturally-minded reader to speak of the resurrection of the body takes its place in describing a far more important subject, the resurrection of the soul. The Lord's words in this respect also "are spirit, and they are life." And each one of us ought to be striving, as the Apostle said, "That I may know Him, and the power of His resurrection, and the fellowship of His sufferings, being made conformable unto His death; if by any means I might attain to the resurrection of the dead. Not as though I had already attained, either were already perfect."—Phil. iii. 10—12. Viewing the regeneration and resurrection of the soul as the grand objects of Gospel care, each passage falls readily into its place, and we learn by them all how to rise from the death of sin to the life of righteousness. They all form a solemn call like that of the Apostle, "Awake, thou that sleepest, and arise from the dead, and Christ shall give thee light."—Eph. v. 14.

Considered in this point of view, we apprehend at once the Divine meaning, when the Lord said, "The hour cometh, and NOW is, when the dead shall hear the voice of the Son of God, and they that hear shall live."—John v. 25. The dead who then heard were those who had been dead in trespasses and sins, but who rose to newness of life. And when the Saviour continues, "Marvel not at this, for the hour is coming in the which all that are in the graves shall hear His voice, and shall come forth; they that have done good unto the resurrection of life, and they that have done evil to the resurrection of damnation"—28, 29; we think of the "graves that appear not"—Luke xi. 44; the "whited sepulchres which appear beautiful without, but within are full of dead men's bones and all uncleanness"—Matt. xxiii. 27; and out of which men must come when they are judged. All appearances are put off, when judgment is executed. The real inner men come forth. "They that have done good to the resurrection of life, and they that have done evil to the resurrection of damnation."

The "vile body," which is fashioned like unto the Lord's

glorious body—Phil. iii. 21—is also the spiritual body, vile by sin in its unregenerate condition, but lighted up with beauty by the glorious working of the Holy Spirit. This too, is the "mortal which puts on immortality, the corruptible which puts on incorruption, when God giveth us the victory through our Lord Jesus Christ, and death is swallowed up in victory"—1 Cor. xv. 54, 55, 57. All becomes harmony when we think of the resurrection of the soul; and he who has attained to this priceless resurrection may with fullest faith exclaim with the Apostle, fearing nothing, doubting nothing: "For we KNOW that if our earthly house of this tabernacle were dissolved, WE HAVE A BUILDING OF GOD, a house not made with hands, eternal in the Heaven. For in this we groan, earnestly desiring to be clothed upon with our house which is from Heaven."—2 Cor. v. 1, 2.

Let us not think, then, that Adam has been waiting somewhere for thousands of years without a body, and not knowing what shape or sort of life he has been in, or is in. Let us not suppose that Job, or any other of the worthies of the Old Testament, have been waiting in a sort of nondescript half-existence without shape, and in a world that has no shape. Oh, no! That is as near nothing as possible. But they have taken with them the real man which has been formed during life, into their everlasting home, where God gives to every man as his work shall be. "Behold, I come quickly," He says; not, "I will let you wait for thousands of years, not knowing what will be your lot, until some judgment at a remote period takes place." You are forming yourselves every day, and judging yourselves. You may, if you look within yourselves, find what you have written there, either good or bad; you may see what you have been, and what you are. That, therefore, is the reason why, if you have been negligent of God's laws, you should now endeavour to live for them. Obedience to right "is no vain thing; it is our life." We are now in the process of being made. We are made in conformity with our life. "They shall come forth; they that have done good unto the resurrection of life, and they that have done evil unto the resurrection of damnation." Death is but the period for the disclosure of our work, fully, fairly, completely, and for ever.

Let us, then, take the glorious assurance of this truth to our hearts, first of all, to make us earnest in endeavouring to live for Heaven: we are living either for Heaven or for hell every day. Let us write upon ourselves the glorious principles that make an angel—"love to God, love to man, heavenly wisdom, constant progress, doing and acting after the Saviour's great example, and by His power;" and when we have written these upon every part of our nature, we are as the Apostle said, "Ye are our epistle." We are, each of us, writing the gospel upon ourselves if we so live. We shall then come forth when health is fading away from us, when the body is becoming feeble and withered like the chaff of the ripened corn; when the chaff falls away, the corn comes out in its perfection; so will it be with us. When our covering falls off, when our sheath becomes chaff, and goes to its mother earth, the spirit will ascend in its glorious beauty to God, who gave it. We shall mingle with those who are like-minded with ourselves, to live to make others happy, each having heaven within himself, and form a part of those who inhabit those "many mansions" which are found in our heavenly "Father's house." We shall enter into a glorious world where all are happy, all are beautiful, all are wise, because all are good.

DISCUSSION.

REV. VICAR OF ——. I should leave this room, Christian friends, in a very different state of feeling, and with very different views to those that I entered it, if the sentiments which have just been broached by the lecturer were scriptural. I believe they are anti-scriptural; and on that account I rise simply to give it as my deliberate opinion, that however honest the lecturer may be, and however anxious he may be to impress upon our minds those things which he regards as truth, I look upon them as directly opposed to what God in His Holy Word has taught us. (Hear.) He has referred over and over again to various passages—sometimes in the Old Testament, and sometimes in the New—and he has laboured to prove that there is no such thing as the resurrection of the body. All that I have to say is this, that if the Apostle Paul, and the other Apostles, and other inspired and holy men in the Old Testament, do not distinctly and emphatically teach the resurrection of the dead, then I neither understand my own language—I know nothing of Hebrew, and still less of Greek. The Apostle, in language, as it appears to me, incontrovertible, does most emphatically and plainly teach, so that the ploughman may understand what the man says. He tells the ploughman—if I have any correct apprehension of what the Apostle of the Gentiles teaches in the sublime and inconceivably beautiful chapter, where he treats of the resurrection of the dead—I say he does there distinctly teach the poor peasant as well as the philosopher, who is oftentimes too wise to be taught, that the body which is sown in corruption will be raised in incorruption, and that which is sown a natural body will be raised a spiritual body. I declare solemnly that I should leave this room a miserable man if I did not believe, not only that my immortal spirit would live for ever in the presence of God, but if I did not also believe that the body in its spiritualized state—not in this gross material form—in that we are all agreed, I think—but that the material body that will be sown in corruption will be raised in incorruption; that is to say, will be raised an incorruptible body, and that this body will be the vehicle of the operations of the immortal spirit. Touching the passage in Job, we know that some have taken one view of that subject, and some another. The Hebrew term, for example, has been rendered "vindicator;" but in my humble judgment, that grand and glorious passage does as distinctly and emphatically teach the resurrection of the dead, as does the Apostle in the beautiful chapter, the 15th of his First Epistle to the Corinthians. There is another sublime and beautiful passage in one of the minor prophets, "I will ransom them from the power of the grave;" but according to the lecturer, if I understand him, there is no grave from which to ransom them—"I will ransom them from the power of the grave; I will redeem them from death: O death, I will be thy plagues; O grave, I will be thy destruction: repentance shall be hid from mine eyes." I could say a great deal more; time, however, is fast proceeding, and I shall now wait to hear what the lecturer feels disposed to say in answer to what I have advanced. (Applause.)

Dr. BAYLEY: In relation to what our friend's opinions and convictions are, as opinions they will depend of course precisely upon the weight that is attached to the arguments he has offered for our attention. Our friend's mere statement, of his convictions being this or that, of course merely announced his conviction. (Hear, hear.) You have heard, during the course of this lecture, some of the reasons for my convictions, which tell me not of the distant resurrection about which our friend has spoken, but of a present resurrection—of our immediate entrance into the fulness of heavenly glory which I believe the Scripture to teach. Our friend has not referred to any of the passages or to the instruction I have offered upon the subject, but simply announced in answer to them his convictions and his opinions, which, of course, will have just the weight that the arguments in support of them have, and nothing more. In relation, first of all, to Job, I pointed out both what the passage really said, and how it was really fulfilled in relation to Job. Our friend has said nothing at all to show that this was not the accurate construction—only that some people think so, and other people think different. But Job tells us in the 10th and 16th chapters, at the end, that when he leaves this world by death, he will not return. I have already quoted Job's declaration, "He that goeth down to the grave shall come up no more." What we hope is, that each of you will read Job carefully—leaving out those words that are in italics—taking in what Job announces as the fulfilment of his hope, that he would see God—and then judge for yourselves which is the right view. (Applause.) The only other passage that our friend has referred to in the Old Testament, is the announcement of Jehovah himself, that He will ransom us from the power of the grave; He will redeem us from death. But the fulfilment of that glorious declaration is not to be waited for yet, as a thing in the far distance. When did the Redeemer come into the world? Has not the Redeemer appeared? Has not He done His work? Did not He come into the world eighteen hundred years ago, and did not He, when He was in the world, say, "He that heareth my word, and believeth on Him that sent me, hath everlasting life, and shall not come into condemnation, but is PASSED from death unto life"? There is the fulfilment of the promise of redemption. ("Doubtful.") What graves are we anxious to be delivered from?—is it not those graves of which He speaks, when He says to the Pharisees, "Ye are like unto whited sepulchres, which indeed appear beautiful outward, but are within full of dead men's bones, and of all uncleanness"? (Applause.) These are the graves, and that is the death that Christ desires to deliver us from. He does not leave it for us to guess whether, in some far distant time, it will be done or not; but He announces that it was done. Every person that comes out of the grave of sin and corruption—out of the death of evil, can say now, "Thanks be to God, who has given us the victory through our Lord Jesus Christ." There is no longer any grave or any death for him; his is already a life that is certain. What did Christ say again? "He that liveth and believeth in me shall never die;" may I not say to my brother, "Believest thou this?" If you believe this, then you believe that the fulfilment of the passage you have referred to has been wrought out, has been amply completed; and you and I have only to rejoice that we are living in the real life, the glorious life of Heaven now, and we shall enter the holier life of eternity at last, when this earthly body is put away. I entered very fully into the 15th of the First Epistle to the Corinthians; all that our friend has replied to what was said, and the words were quoted and dwelt upon, is to misquote one little passage. He says that we shall be sown in corruption and will be raised in incorruption. That is not what the Apostle says—he says, "It is sown in corruption, and is raised in incorruption;" not "will be." That "will be" is altogether of our friend's introducing; it does not occur in the Scriptures. (Hear, hear.) The Scriptures say, "There is a natural body, and there is a spiritual body." Now our friend talked about Hebrew and Greek—it only needs plain English to know that "is," does not mean "will be." It is quite as plain in the Hebrew and Greek as it is in the English. The plain English is precisely as it is rendered, and as it *ought* to be rendered. There is now a natural body, and there is now a spiritual body. It is the natural body that is sown, and it is the spiritual body that is raised. That is precisely our doctrine, and we have been teaching this through the whole lecture. I am sure that although our friend thinks that he would be a sadder man if he took this doctrine, I can assure him from experience he is mistaken. I have been in his state, I have had his doctrine; but now I have this doctrine, and it makes me a happier man. It would be to me a sadness—I should be grievously sad—if when I saw my dear ones go away from my side, I had an idea that they were going to be a sort of half nothing, in no shape, and no where; to wait for some thousands of years till it was settled where they were to go. Our friend thinks there is to be a future very distant judgment, whenever it may come. If I thought so, it would make me very sad. I am, however, certain as the fullest investigation can make me, that every one who has had a true devotion to his Lord, who has lived for Christ in this world—I have not the slightest doubt that when they pass from among the abodes of men, they go in bodies more perfect, more glorious, and more beautiful, at once, to the abode of angels; and that makes me happy. (Loud cheers.) It is a happy thing for me to think that those whom I have loved here, and striven to make happy, go to better hands than mine; that they have not to wait in any half existence, or no existence; but as for them to live is Christ, so for them to die is gain. I feel sure that if our friend gives himself the attentive examination that so weighty a matter requires, he will find there will be no loss of happiness, but great gain, in the reception of this advanced view of the Sacred Word.

REV. VICAR: Nothing that has been advanced by the chairman in the shape of replication, has in the least altered my views or my feelings. It appears to me almost beyond —I was going to say—contempt, that he should have stated that I quoted a passage incorrectly for the sake of impressing my view. I know as well as the lecturer that the Apostle's words are, "It is sown in corruption; it is raised in incorruption." Why the material body, flesh and blood, is sown in corruption, and it is raised in incorruption. And I believe all the sophistry, and all the eloquence, and all the false logic, and all the Biblical criticism, which he, or any other man, can bring to bear upon that passage, or the whole of that inimitably sublime composition of the great Apostle of the Gentiles, will fail, and fail to the end of time, to prove that he has there spoken of mere spiritual resurrection; he is speaking, if I understand human language, of the general resurrection from the dead. I believe, as well as the lecturer, that dear friends who die sleep in Jesus —go to heaven. I believe their spirits enter an ineffably blessed state, and that they are not in some far distant region, wondering—if they have the power to wonder—when the resurrection is to take place, and what they are to be. Mothers who lose their darling children, may rejoice in the thought that they are gone to be with Jesus; but their bodies, as well as their spirits, will be with Jesus—that is their resurrection body. There is no language, I conceive, in the whole of the New Testament, for the lecturer to put the matter in the way he has done. It appears to me not at all Christian. He says this is my opinion; and I suppose every man and every woman in the United Kingdom has a right to his or her opinion. It is the opinion of the Universal Church—it is the opinion of the first philosophers that have ever existed, that our bodies shall all be raised. Why is a man to be punished solely in his spirit, seeing that its partner—the body—has been one great instrument and cause of sin? I want to know how that which has sinned in many, many instances, is to receive no punishment? or how that which has been active in the service of God, is to receive no reward?

Another friend (Mr. WILKINS, Baptist minister): Whatever the decision of this meeting will be, it will not affect the thing itself. There is one thing that has struck me forcibly, and that is in reference to the resurrection of our Lord Jesus Christ: if He has risen from the dead, which certainly He has; and if He has become the firstfruits of them that slept; and if He is gone into the invisible world—into the heaven of heavens, as a pattern of what His Church is to be—I want to know how we shall resemble Him, unless our bodies are raised as His body was? Jesus Christ said, "Handle me and see; for a spirit hath not flesh and blood, as ye see me have." (Hear, hear.) Now, if Jesus Christ be a pattern of His Church, which certainly He is, how can we imitate Him, unless our bodies are raised like His? (Applause.)

DR. BAYLEY: Allow me first to answer my first friend. Although I do not know that he has presented any new argument—only the very strong declaration of its being his opinion—that the apostle meant so and so. He admitted that the correction which I made of his quotation was a correct rendering, and he said he knew it. Our friend, perhaps, might feel a little hurt from his supposing that I meant to insinuate that he intentionally misquoted a passage for a certain purpose. I did not mean to insinuate anything of the kind, but simply that when we have been used to a certain doctrine, and suppose it to be in a certain part of the Scriptures, we unconsciously quote the Scriptures as we have been in the habit of doing, although, perhaps, mistakenly. Many people quote the Scriptures as they have been used to them, but never have their attention directed to see what the Word exactly says. What it exactly says in this case, is what I have been saying all night—that we have a spiritual body as well as a natural body, and that the natural body is sown, and the spiritual body is raised. Now that is precisely what we need to take home with us, and then we shall have all the requirements for a true idea of spiritual life. Our friend has offered an argument, not a Scriptural one, but an argument which has sometimes been proposed before—namely, that as the body has sinned, why should not the body be punished as well as the soul? and this argument seems to have some little weight in it, only that it would go farther than those who use it would intend it to go: for it would go thus far—if the body is really wanted to bear part in either the reward or punishment, why is not it taken when the soul is taken? (Cheers.) Why does not it go, at the same time as the soul, if it is to be happy in heaven? Nay, why not all the bodies? But the reason is evident. The body is only an instrument in the soul's hands. The body never sinned in its life. (Loud cheers.) It is the soul that sins. A man might as well say when a horse has run away with the cart, the cart is as bad as the horse, and whip them both. (Hear, hear.) He might as well say that because an assassin uses a pistol to murder a person, and he is hung for the crime, that you should hang the pistol as well as the man. Our friend's arguments—I say it with all respect—are as weak as water. I have no doubt that he is quite aware of the present condition of science, and knows that the body is being changed continually; so that we have a dozen bodies if we live to be old men. Would he say that these bodies are all to be brought up? These are things our friend would do well to take into consideration. (Friend: "Thank you," sarcastically.)

As to the soundest philosophers who thought in this way; he knows surely that what we teach, the present philosophers teach—(Friend: "Present infidels, you mean!")—the old philosophers, who had a philosophy as false as the old notions of the Scriptures were, might have taught as our friend does. But Sir Humphrey Davy was no infidel, and he taught precisely what we teach in relation to the body—that it is changed every day, and that it would be no more wrong to punish the whip than it would be to punish the body. Tillotson taught it, and he was no infidel, but an archbishop. Watts taught it. I would say further, that there is not a leading philosopher of the present day that does not teach the same thing. I will invite our friend to try if he can find a philosopher of any name whatever, within the last twenty years, that does not teach what we teach. Let him then uphold, if he will, the old philosophy; but let us seek for the true philosophy, founded on facts, which has advanced something higher and grander and nobler than that of bygone days.

And now I will address our second friend. Many have regarded this as an evidence, as our friend has, that inasmuch as Christ rose with His body, therefore our natural bodies will rise too. But the apostle says, "Every man in his own order." Jesus rose, and we shall rise, but every man in his own order; and the "order" of Jesus is that He was Governor of heaven and earth. "All power is given unto Him in heaven and in earth." His body inwardly was an incorruptible body; it was the "Word from His Divine soul made flesh:" His body was gradually glorified and perfected. The glorious form that appeared on mount Tabor, when "His face did shine as the sun," that was His real body within the form from Mary. Besides what men saw, there was another Divine form continually expanding itself until, when He arose, His body was perfectly Divine, like His soul. "I do cures to-day, and to-morrow, and the third day I shall be perfected." His risen body could move in and out of houses without the doors being opened—a body that those who had their spiritual sight open could see; but no common Jew, with only his natural eye, saw His body after His resurrection. His body, therefore, was a Divine body; but ours is only an earthly one, suited to this world; —and, therefore, He rose in His own order; as the glorious God that had to rule heaven and earth, but had glorified and perfected His body while He lived in the world, and now from that glorious body governs heaven and earth. Jesus took His body with Him. Our body is not the "word made flesh;" our bodies are merely the outward corruptible forms that pass into dust. "Every man in his own order." We do not want these bodies, and so we leave them behind us. He wanted His, and so He took it with Him. That is my answer to our second friend.

SECOND FRIEND: If his answer proves anything it proves that it was by death and by the resurrection that the body of Jesus became what it really was; so that it could pass from place to place without hindrance. If, as the lecturer has told us, the body of Christ was Divine, then Divinity can bleed and die;—the body of Christ bled and died. The lecturer has been telling us that His body was made Divine; if that be true, His body was perfectly Divine before His death. As I have said, if that argument shows anything, it goes to prove that Divinity must die, because Jesus Christ bled and died. I do not see how the lecturer can prove from that, in any measure, that our body is not to be raised. After the resurrection, Jesus Christ went in and out unseen; but before death He went about with the disciples, and was seen as we are. The change was after the resurrection of Christ, just as the change will be with us. I can say with our friend who has spoken on the subject, in reply to the lecturer, that the body is sown in corruption, and raised in incorruption. As this is a subject so vast and of so much importance, I will endeavour to give my views more fully on Sunday evening next, at the Queen Square Baptist Chapel; and I shall be glad to see as many of my friends as possible on that occasion.

FIRST FRIEND: Bacon, the great experimental philosopher, Boyle, Sir Isaac Newton, "not less than the least of philosophers,"—these men died, and were buried in a certain hope of a resurrection of their bodies into everlasting life.

DR. BAYLEY: I have only to remark further, that I am exceedingly obliged to the gentlemen who have placed these matters before us, and to the one who seems likely to make them still more interesting, by turning the attention of the people to them on Sunday night. I hope there will be many present, that there will be an earnest and interesting examination of the subject, and that we shall endeavour to "prove all things, and hold fast that which is good." Our respected friend has named some of the philosophers; which he, I suppose, has done, because of my referring to the philosophy of the present day; but without quoting even what the philosophers have said on the subject before us. It is very possible that had he done so, he would have found they would have been like Locke, who was a great philosopher, and who taught precisely as we teach, and in a very contrary sense to what our friend has named. When he brings up any argument from Newton, or Boyle, we shall be very glad to attend to the argument, and to see whether there is anything in it, and to give it all the weight that a respectable proposition ought to have at all times. For anything else but argument, I assure him, we have no respect. Anything that our friend has to say about demeanour and so on, will be better left to those who hear to judge. (Hear, hear.) I have tried to give, at least a respectable and courteous hearing to what has been brought before us. (Cheers.) I will just add a word or two to our friend's (the Rev. Mr. Wilkins) remarks, which may assist him not to misrepresent our ideas. Our doctrine is—that the Lord through life, and at death, was going through a work of perfecting and glorifying His humanity. That at the beginning there was within the human nature from Mary, a germ of the Divine nature from God Himself—that "holy thing" that was born was the Son of God within' as was there the Son "made of a woman" without. This Divine nature in the human was being more fully brought out during the Saviour's life; but the mere human from Mary remained so far that it might be crucified, and it was crucified. It was not the Divine body that was crucified or died. I hope our friend, in stating his ideas, will keep to what we assure him are our views upon the subject. It was the human from Mary which suffered and died, but there had been from the first gradually expanding a Divine humanity, from Himself, and that was the Son seen on mount Tabor, when "His raiment was white as the light." The Divine body from within was that which rose, the glorious, the perfect body; and which John saw, when he beheld the First and the Last.

THE FIFTH LECTURE.

JUDGMENT, INDIVIDUAL AND GENERAL.

"It is appointed unto men once to die, but after this the judgment."—Heb. ix. 27.

"Now is the judgment of this world; now shall the prince of this world be cast out."—John xii. 31.

PRAYER BEFORE THE LECTURE.

O LORD, our adorable Saviour and Judge, to whom our hearts and works are known, be present, inspire, and guide all our deliberations. Without Thee we can know nothing true, and do nothing good. Be within us, Gracious Lord, the hope of glory, the light of faith, and the strength of virtue. From Thy Divine love, create in us the love of Thy commandments. Make our affections free from the love of self, and every evil motive; and as Thou Thyself wilt try the heart and reins of all Thy children, prepare us to stand in Thy sight, O Thou Most Holy, and hear Thy gracious words to each of us, "Well done, thou good and faithful servant, enter thou into the joy of thy Lord." These mercies we ask, Lord Jesus, in Thy own sacred name, and for Thy loving-kindness sake.

LECTURE.

THE subject appointed for our consideration to-night is that of Judgment—first individual, and then general—including replies to the important questions, When is man judged? and, Where is man judged?

Before passing to our main topic, however, allow me just to make a remark or two in relation to another which has been introduced by a friend, who kindly offered his arguments on the Resurrection the other evening, and more at large on Sunday evening last, who has also presented us with them in a printed form. I wish just to say a word or two to one who has felt it his duty to stand up for what he believes to be the truth of God, and is on that account worthy of all respect. I shall not divert you from the argument of this evening any more than is necessary, not only because it would be unprofitable to do so, but also because I had the advantage of the arguments offered by our friend, in sufficient time to write out a short reply to them, without mentioning his name; for we are of those who believe that charity and love are greater than ideas, or even than truth. And sometimes a gentleman is hurt by the use of his name; particularly if attached to what turns out to be a very poor argument. The cause of truth obtains nothing from personalities. You will have our friend's arguments presented in his sermon for a penny; you will have the way in which we regard those arguments in a sort of nut-shell condition, for half the sum. And perhaps you will have the goodness to compare them together, and to "prove all things, and hold fast that which is good." There is one additional remark which I deem it necessary to make, and that is in relation to what our friend, in the early part of his discourse, was tempted to name the "sophistical manner" in which the arguments we had offered were presented to the public. Now, I wish to assure our friend that although the arguments may appear to him to be unsound, they are sincere. He has a perfect right to have his own opinion upon that subject—but every other person has the same right. The humblest man amongst us has a right as a Protestant,—and especially all who think with my friend, as Dissenters,—must grant that others have a right to their opinion; to hold that which seems to them the true; to hold it firm and fast because it is the truth. And God speed all in the use of this right: long may they be enabled by its use to become free, thoughtful, rational Christians. But, at the same time, allow me to remind our friend and others, that we also claim the same right. (Applause.) We, too, are Protestants; we, too, claim the privilege of holding our opinions, of presenting our arguments, of delivering them to others, as we find we have opportunity. We also hold that we ought to use this privilege, not only as a right, but a right to be used charitably. We suppose that others in advocating their views are as sincere as we are; but we beg others to believe that WE ARE AS SINCERE AS THEY ARE. (Applause.) Our salvation is as dear to us as their salvation is to them. We believe our salvation will be obtained only by the truth; and if any one can point out to us that either arguments or statements which we rely upon are not true, we give them up immediately. But when a person, not satisfied with his success in argument, insinuates that we are not sincere—that we are "sophistical;" that we are trying to make a thing which we know to be false appear to be true, we say, as our Lord says, "Judge not, that ye be not judged." By his own master must every man stand or fall. I hope the hint thus given will prevent my friend in future, however unsatisfactory he may contend our arguments are, from assuming the place of judge, for which no mortal is fitted, and pronouncing them "sophistical."

Let us now advance to the consideration of the great theme before us; and, first of all, to the judgment of each individual, which takes place with every man, as we conceive, immediately after death. Here allow me to observe upon the treatment which reason obtains from Old Church advocates which, although not exclusively connected with the subject before us, is very commonly manifested, and which I find in the sermon to which I have slightly adverted. When any one undertakes to show that one of the common doctrines is unreasonable—although we generally find that people are exceedingly glad to make use of reason whenever it can be got to be on their side—yet, when a doctrine is found to be unreasonable, and the person who holds it cannot show that it is not so, it is a very common thing for him to begin to hold forth about mysteries which he declares are above man's comprehension, and to say that they are too high for reason—that they appear to us to be contradictory—but, in some mysterious way, they are, nevertheless, true, because they are great mysteries. Why, this argument is REASONING. They are reasoning when they tell us not to reason. For such arguments we have no respect. We venerate no man's nonsense because he calls it a mystery, and asserts that it is above our reason. Mysteries—true mysteries—God's mysteries, are not things that are contradictory, or that can be shown to be contradictory. They are hidden wisdom; they are deeper truths than usual; they are things that you are invited to think about, not to shun; and when by meditation you understand them—when you behold their real nature and character, you will find that they are always grander wisdom than any other of God's lessons. The mysteries of God are not contradictory, but are higher disclosures of holy wisdom. It is man-made mysteries that are contradictory. Mysteries in religion are what the Apostle Paul speaks of when he says, "Though I have the gift of prophecy, and UNDERSTAND all mysteries, and have not charity, I am nothing." Divine mysteries are such as can be understood, if a man will apply himself to them, and go on seeking the truth till the truth opens upon him in all its harmony and glory. "It is given unto you to KNOW the mysteries of the kingdom of heaven," said the Lord Jesus. The Apostle Paul says, "Howbeit we speak the wisdom of God in a mystery, even the hidden wisdom which God ordained before the world."—1 Cor. ii. 7; thus teaching that the mystery of God is hidden wisdom. Again, he says, "Whereby, when ye read, ye may understand my knowledge in the mystery of Christ; which in other ages was not made known unto the sons of men, but IS NOW REVEALED unto His holy apostles and prophets by the Spirit."—Eph. iii. 4, 5; thus informing us that what had formerly been a mystery, was now revealed. And once more, he says, "And to make all men see what is the fellowship of the mystery, which from the beginning of the world hath been hid in God, who created all things by Jesus Christ (the Word made flesh) : to the intent that now unto the principalities and powers in heavenly places might be known by the church the manifold wisdom of God."—Eph. iii. 9, 10. Here that which had been a mystery when hid, was, when discovered, the manifold wisdom of God. Such are all Divine mysteries. Contradictions are only human mysteries, and are, strictly speaking, only pious frauds.

And when a person tells me something that I see to be utterly irrational—which amounts to this, that a thing IS and IS NOT at the same time—when a person tells me that in a certain matter three times one make one—when a person tells me that a bit of bread, which he has got from a baker's shop, or made himself, is the great God who fills heaven and earth—when a person tells me that the same body which is buried will be raised, but it won't be the same, it will be spiritual—when it is said these and similar things must be believed, however contradictory, because they are mysteries above our reason, I say, excuse me, they are not above reason in the least; they are far below and contrary to reason.

All truth will be found to come out right when tried in a threefold manner. Three classes of truth all come from God. All truths will be found right if tried by Scripture;

they will be found right if tried by reason; they will be right if tried by science. Reason, Scripture, and science all come from God, and in Him harmonise; and they must harmonise if we get them right from Him. Therefore, if a man tells me that he has something that is very spiritual and sublime, but is unreasonable and unscientific, I know he is mistaken: it does not stand the threefold test. But a man will say, perhaps, the Scripture says so and so—although no man can truly say the Scripture teaches that dead bodies shall rise. He may draw inferences from the letter of the sacred Scriptures because there is what is called the "letter that killeth," as well as "the spirit that giveth life." And if a man take some portion of the sacred Scriptures, and use it without reference to their spirit and life, he may prove many things most absurd. The question is not what the Scripture says only, but what it means. That is the question to be settled. When God gives us Scripture, He not only tells us to read, but He says, "Understandest thou what thou readest?" And if we do not understand, and understand each new truth in harmony with all other truths which we know, we are reading without profit. Hear, again, what He says—"When any one heareth the word of the kingdom and understandeth it not, then cometh the wicked one and catcheth away that which was sown in his heart." Those things that are brought forth under the pretence of being great mysteries, but which persons cannot understand, depend upon it are not from God; they are something man-made. God says, "Come and let us reason together."— Isa. i. 18; and when you have got God's idea, you will find that it is reasonable, it is scientific, and it is scriptural. Thus it comes out with the threefold test by which all doctrine should be tried. Take this idea with you, and you will find you have a light opening upon you as to the mode in which you should treat the sacred Scriptures. You will never have to tell people that a view is scriptural but not rational. If it is really found out to be not rational, or not scientific, it is not because the Scriptures are wrong, but because man's interpretation of them has been mistaken. Well, thus "prove all things;" and how can a person prove all things when he does not use his reason, and "hold fast that which is good"?

We come now, then, to the immediate subject of to-night—individual judgment. This is the first idea to which this evening we wish to call your attention. What we have already said about sound reason and rational science being in harmony with true religion and with the Word of God, when it is rightly understood, belongs to this subject as well as to every other. I have no doubt but that all my respected hearers have oftentimes been told that there is to be a day at some future distant time, when all persons are to be judged; when the Saviour of the world is to come for judgment in the outward clouds of the air. It used to be said that it was to be in the valley of Jehoshaphat, a small valley near to Jerusalem, and that the myriads of human beings who had lived from the beginning of the world up to that period were to be collected in that place, and were there all to be judged. When the judgment was over, the world in which we live was to be burnt up, and all the starry bodies were to partake in the annihilation. But what was to follow after was never very clearly stated. Some thought there was to be another earth and another sky in which the redeemed were to live. Now, notwithstanding you have been told this, and it has been the constant doctrine, very likely preached to most of you for a long time, and from which you would conclude that there was to be no going to heaven or going to hell before the judgment was over, because people were not to be tried until that time. If any went to heaven before, it must be that either they would go on speculation, or else there was somehow to be a trial before; yet it has quite as much been generally preached and supposed that people go to heaven or to hell when they died also. But this is just the sort of thing which we have pointed out in relation to other doctrines. There is to be a grand trial when the world comes to its end, but nevertheless people are to go to heaven and hell when they die besides. If they are judged as soon as they die, and go to heaven directly, what then is the use of that judgment some thousands of years to come? What is the necessity for it? They are judged already, according as we teach and you admit; and why, then, after they have been thousands of years in heaven, and others thousands of years in hell, are they to be brought up, and a form of trial to be gone through? The two things are inconsistent. Can it be to ascertain whether they ought to have been there or not? It is irreverent to think so. Every person surely goes to heaven who ought to go there, and every person goes to hell that ought to go there, and that soon after death. Does it not, then, seem unreasonable to bring them from their everlasting abodes some thousands of years after, and try them over again? Put these two things together, and does the idea look reasonable? Is it a rational doctrine? Are we to be told that this is a great mystery too, and quite above our reason? Are we again to be told we must not inquire into it because it is a great mystery? But this is precisely in the same category with every other of those dark doctrines which were really hatched in times of ignorance and darkness. Let us then inquire, not only what the Scriptures say, but whether the Scriptures mean what persons who have got their doctrine through the dark ages say. Are there really no higher, no brighter views than those which have been handed to us through the dark ages of a dark and fallen church, in which, for superstition's sake, all mysteries were cherished? We believe that better may be had at the present time. We have no reverence for anything because it was professed five hundred or a thousand years ago. If age is the only claim it has, except that persons with great names, in those days of pride and selfishness, held such doctrines. We have not the slightest reverence for them on these accounts. If they had good reasons for holding their doctrines, we ask, What were their reasons? Give us the reasons; never mind the names. If the thing is right, we hold to it for that reason; if the thing is wrong and pernicious—if it tends to make us such-like Christians only as these men, called Christians, were, a thousand or even three hundred years ago, we shall be content to go without their doctrines and their light. The church of those times was a stupid, absurd, dark, persecuting, vicious church, and the less we go back to it the better. We must go on. Churches never go back. God never goes back in nature or in spirit. We are not to go back to Judaism, nor to the dark ages of Christianity. God has promised that there will come a time in which a new city—a city of heavenly gold, and clear as crystal—will come down from Him, in which principles will be revealed that will make religion clear. "The time cometh when I shall show you plainly of the Father"—John xvi. 25. There will be a time in which religion will be found to be such that men shall know the Lord all over the earth. "The earth shall be full of the knowledge of the Lord, as the waters cover the sea." And we say to men, go on; don't go back, neither to the old mummery of three hundred, or seven hundred, or fifteen hundred years ago; but look up to the living God of this age. Look to Him as your Divine teacher; let His word harmoniously teach you, and then you will find that sound religion, sound rationality, and sound science all go hand in hand together. They all come from the same God, and all alike tend to make us noble-minded men.

Well, we have named the inconsistency which comes out in this notion of having two judgments—two general judgments; first of all letting persons go some to heaven and others to hell, and then trying them thousands of years after, to ascertain whether they ought to have gone to their several places or not. We must surely see this as a subject which requires a little more light. Then we come to the notion about there being a last day for this outward universe, in which the stars are to fall from heaven, and then come down to the earth—although there are millions of suns and worlds, as it is now known: and even one of our planets,

Jupiter, is as large as nine hundred earths, if they were all rolled into one. I say, although persons have had this notion, whatever becomes of it, we are certain that the doctrine of the sacred Scriptures is that each person's probation is finished when he has worked out his salvation, or refused his salvation, at the end of his life in the world. That is his last day—the individual last day; and Christ raises him up at his last day, to enter, if he be prepared for heaven, into the abodes of the blessed. Jesus says, "I am the resurrection and the life;" not "I shall be thousands of years hence," but "I am." And every person who puts off his earthly covering is drawn by the spirit of Jesus into the eternal world, and there associated with his own heaven, if he is prepared for heaven, if not, not. "And I," He says, "if I be lifted up, will draw all men unto me."

This is the doctrine of the sacred Scriptures throughout. Any one who reads our Lord's words in relation to death at any time, will find that man's final state is then realised. "Behold!" He says, "I COME QUICKLY, and my reward is with me:" not, behold, you are to wait for thousands of years: "Behold, I come quickly, and my reward is with me, to give every man as his work shall be"—Rev. xxii. 12. Again, says the same Divine Teacher, when He is likening men to the labourers in a vineyard, "When even was come, the lord of the vineyard saith unto his steward, Call the labourers, and give them their hire, beginning from the last unto the first"—Matt. xx. 8. He does not say that the day was closed then; but there was an immense gap yet to be passed, for no purpose—a sort of half-existence, in which, unless they have what my friend calls in his sermon that indefinable body, the spiritual body, we know not what they are. Our friend has not given much attention to spiritual bodies and spiritual things, evidently; and therefore he regards the spiritual body as an indefinable body. There is nothing more indefinable about it, however, than about the natural body. "There is a natural body, and there is a spiritual body." A body is an external, fitted to the world in which it lives. The body which is fitted to this natural world, is a natural body; the body that is fitted to the other world is a spiritual body. It is quite as easy to understand one as it is to understand the other; and when the spiritual body which we have now is regenerated, the Apostle says, "God giveth it a body as it hath pleased Him, and to every seed his own body,"—when this spiritual body has been wrought out, has been made beautiful by the reception of angelic principles, it stands forth in angelic loveliness. This is taught in the sacred Scriptures. The Psalmist says, " I shall be satisfied, when I awake, with Thy likeness;" not satisfied when he awakes, having no shape, or awakes at some enormously distant period, in his old body, in the Lord's likeness; but when he awakes, having gone asleep in time, when he awakes in eternity, with the beauty of the Lord his God upon him, he will be satisfied, he will have every wish fulfilled, a fulness of joy. We cannot suppose that those saints that have gone before us are unsatisfied because they have not got that earthly shell they have left behind them—that they are lingering and hoping and wishing that these shall be brought up. I have looked through the mummies of three or four thousand years ago, which are to be seen in the Egyptian Galleries of the British Museum —those misreable masses of filth and corruption—and thought of a glorious angel like the one which spoke to St. John—who was so magnificent that the Apostle was about to adore him, but was told he must not do it, for he was one of his brethren—and I have asked myself, Can it take anything from the glory of such a blessed one to be without this mass that is here? Let those miserable men who love their bodies so well as to have every care for them, and very little for their souls, look there, and see what they become, notwithstanding all that can be done to preserve them. Can a blessed one—can one who in angelic beauty has been living for thousands of years—can he want this miserable stuff? Oh, no! oh, no! The spirit went to God who gave it; but the dust to dust. "Dust thou art," is said of the body, "and unto dust shalt thou return." We shall be satisfied when we awake in God's likeness. God's likeness is being wrought in us now. The Apostle says, "He that hath wrought us for the self-same thing is God." We are being wrought now. From the first moment that the glorious seeds of truth and goodness from the Lord Jesus Christ enter into our souls, there comes a tinge of spiritual beauty upon them. If we saw man in his natural state, such as God sees him, we should know that he is really as he is described in the Scriptures: "From the sole of the foot even unto the head there is no soundness in it; but wounds, and bruises, and putrifying sores."—Isaiah i. 6. We must be born again. It is not a thing of which there is no necessity. It is not enough if at the last moment we believe in Christian doctrine—believe that our Lord Jesus Christ has died for us, and has done everything for us. We must believe that; but believe in time to let him do the same thing for us that He has done for the world. Your little world has to have new light poured into it; you have to be redeemed from your sins, as He redeemed the world from the power of hell. It is this confusing of two grand truths, and putting them in antagonism one to another, that has led to religion being emasculated of its strength—to its being almost a nullity—a faith alone, instead of a faith in Christ, as our real Saviour, who saves from the sins of passion, of lust, and of selfishness. These are the things that make men unhappy. These are what the world needs saving from. Christ has done His part. "Thou shalt call his name Jesus," says the angel, "for He shall save His people from their sins;" not from the guilt of sin only— not from the punishment of sin only, but He saves from sin itself; and when that is obliterated from a man, he need not concern himself about punishment; it is all over. He is not the man to be punished; he is a new man; he has been born again; and being a new man, and born again by the great Saviour's operation, let him go on rising from the dead and being perfected in heavenly life. This is the real and important resurrection, brethren. We are "dead in trespasses and sins" to begin with, in our religious life; and the grand business for us is to awake, to rouse ourselves; not as my friend has made it out, in part of his sermon—awake out of the earthly dust; but, as the Apostle Paul says, "Awake thou that sleepest, and arise from the dead, and Christ shall give thee light." It is the dust the serpent feeds on we are to awake out of; the dust of ignorance and sensuality. The other dust will do us little harm. You will be quite right if you get the holiness of Jesus Christ formed in you by being born again. The Apostle Paul, in the Epistle to the Philippians, says, "For me to live is Christ, and to die is gain." He had no notion that death for him was any curse; it was a gain. It is only a curse to wicked men, it is a gain to good men. The caterpillar enters upon a better life when it puts off its old case; and when the angel within a man puts off his case, he turns out in the beauty of an angel. "For me to live is Christ, and to die is gain." Paul says, "I press toward the mark for the prize of the high calling of God in Christ Jesus;" "If by any means I might attain unto the resurrection of the dead; not as though I had already attained;" but he was thinking of a very different resurrection from the resurrection of dead bodies. "Not as though I had already attained;" but "if by any means I might attain to the resurrection of the dead," and be conformable to the image of His death. —iii. 10, 11. This is the great resurrection. Let a man go on being thus conformed, and he will be conformed by the spirit of Jesus Christ in proportion as he obeys Him in putting down everything that is opposite to love to God and charity to man—in obeying God's commandments. "If ye love me," the Lord Jesus says, "keep my commandments." "If a man love me, he will keep my words." If we do this, "Christ in us, the hope of glory," will every day make us more like Himself, and this likeness to Himself will begin to shed its holy influence; will make it shine even through the body. It will be seen in your face—it will be seen in your works—it will be seen in the sphere round about you—it will be seen in your temper—it will be seen in the heavenly justice that governs you in every transaction—it will be seen that you are Christ's, and taking His image and likeness upon you, become truly a Christ's-man. That is the meaning of the word "Christian," Christ's-man. He only is a true Christian who is Christ's-man; he only who has "Christ in him, the hope of glory," being worked out every day, will, when he comes to the termination of his day's work—the end of his regenerate life, when his work is finished—he will not have to wait for his crown. Having been the soldier of Christ, fighting against sin, "wrestling against spiritual wickedness in high places"—having taken "the sword of the spirit, which is the Word of God," and used it against his evils of temper, and of every other kind, against everything he finds not in harmony with the spirit of Christ—having fought as a good soldier of Christ, day after day, when he comes to the end of his life's campaign, he will find the "crown of righteousness" there. It has not to be waited for during thousands of years. "Be thou faithful unto death," says the Lord Jesus, "and I will give thee a crown of life;" not thou shalt wait an immense period and then shalt possess it. The beggar who lay at the rich man's gate, subject to contumely and scorn, was, nevertheless, Christ's man in his degree. "The beggar died, and was carried by the angels into Abraham's bosom." No waiting—no long interval—was carried instantly. Why, what would he have to wait for? The grave effects nothing: People in the dark ages used to think in this way: God was something like themselves; and as they had great imperfections of memory, God also, they thought, would forget if He did not keep a great book, and so he employed the angels as book-keepers; and when any person committed a fault, it had to be written down in this book; and angels were employed in this strange business. Everybody, it was believed, would have to be judged out of this great book. But what a narrow idea of God was this! As if He needed

to be reminded by writing in a book what had happened at
a certain time, or as if He needed witnesses; He who knows
all things from the beginning. He would certainly never
give the angels the employment of taking notes in this way.
It was a puny, narrow, conceited, self-derived notion, as to
what is meant by writing in books in the Scriptures. Daniel
says he saw when the judgment was set, he had a vision;
his spiritual sight was opened, and he saw into the eternal
world; he beheld the representation of the judgment going
on, as you will read in Daniel vii. 10, 11, "And the Ancient
of days did sit; thousand thousands ministered unto Him,
and ten thousand times ten thousand stood before him; the
judgment was set, and the books were opened." But what
books? Every man's mind is his book. "Your sin," says
Jeremiah in the seventeenth chapter and first verse, "Your
sin is written with a pen of iron and with the point of a
diamond; it is graven upon the table of your heart, and
upon the horns of your altars." That is where sin is written.
God's laws are always so perfect that they execute themselves. He is not like imperfect men. He has not to make
a law, and then appoint some one to look after it to see that
it is carried into effect. God's laws are always self-vindi-
cating. Let the wicked man try ever so much, he cannot
avoid being his own book-keeper. Let him try to conceal
as much as he pleases, and yet the mark will be made upon
his own soul. It is there; he knows it is. There is not
one of us but who can turn over the pages of the book of the
soul, and tell what is written there. And that which we try
to conceal the most, will be written the plainest. The soul
of each person is his book. Sin makes its impressions and
workings upon the soul when we cherish it. The cunning
man—the person who is continually scheming in order
to get some selfish end, he forms his spirit in a fox-like
manner, until you can see the fox peering out of his eyes;
you may see the cunning in everything he does. The wolfish
man is continually working out in himself the desire of
trampling upon others. But the violence of the passions

which so awfully affect others affect himself still worse. We need to learn fully these truths, brethren—they are our life. We have overlooked these things too much, and leaned upon a sham religion that has had nothing in it. We want a true religion which goes hand in hand with knowing the principles that regenerate a man—knowing what heaven and hell are, and knowing that we are living every day for either the one or the other. There is no mistake about it. We can go and find incipient heavens and hells upon earth. We can go into our own neighbourhoods, and see the hells of that neighbourhood. Those that are infernally-minded are miserable in themselves, and they make others miserable around. They are demons already—half, or three-quarters, or nearly full blown, until at length they will become so malignant, and so blind, and so stupid, as to be mad with their insanity—be indeed insane from the principles they have loved and cherished. That is what is meant in the Sacred Scriptures, where hell is described not only as a place of fire, but also as a place of darkness. A person that thinks merely according to the letter of the Scriptures, if he thinks at all, would be puzzled with this contrariety. A very large number of persons think very little, alas, about religion or anything else. Our efforts are sometimes useful in rousing people to think, but are most useful when we can draw them to spiritual truth. Spiritual truths speak to us by experience. They furnish their own evidence. When a person is in a passion, he is not only on fire with fury, but he becomes blind with foolishness. You will never interest a person when he is in a passion. He is sure to judge wrongly, because his mind is as dark and foolish as his heart is mad. The Scriptures, when understood in relation to man's interior state, always give us clear and important lessons. On the other hand, a person who loves the things of heaven—who loves goodness because it comes from God, who is supremely good; who loves the truth because it comes from God, and is a light in the soul; who shows his love to those by really obeying them in life,—such a person becomes heavenly-minded. "The kingdom of God," says our blessed Saviour, "is within you." You see he already possesses the spirit of heaven, in the gentleness, the kindness, the self-sacrifice, and the willingness to do whatever the will of God teaches should be done to promote the happiness of those around him. And such a man will be a little heaven—such a man knows he is going to heaven, because he has heaven in him. This is the real preparation, the real thing that is required to be effected by the power of religion in every soul. They go to heaven, who have received heaven into themselves. If a person has obtained the heaven of loving God and his neighbour, he will show it from the beginning of the day onwards, in whatever he has to do. Such a person is prepared for heaven, and heaven is prepared for him. Well, when he is thus prepared, is it not a welcome doctrine as well as the doctrine of the sacred Scriptures—that when his talents have thus been used, whether the two have made other two, or whether the five have made other five—our Lord will say immediately, "Well done, good and faithful servant; thou hast been faithful over a few things, I will make thee ruler over many things: enter thou into the joy of thy Lord." He is prepared for heaven, and he goes. His character has been formed by his works, and is heavenly. The Christian is what his spirit is. If he is thus built up for heaven by a living obedience to the Lord Jesus, he feels the attraction to heaven, and heaven feels welcome to him. He dies like Lazarus, and is carried by the angels into Abraham's bosom.

The angels had doubtless been round him long before. It is a matter we very often forget, that the spirit-world is not at an immense distance. Men have thought, since they got so immersed in the concerns of their bodies, that there was nothing else but body in the world. That was the idea which almost spread over mankind years ago, and many are labouring under it still. Sometimes, it is true, in words they confess something else, they talk about going to heaven and glory, and so on; and about, immediately when they die, getting to "Canaan's happy shore." But when you seek to understand them on the matter, you will find there is no very definite idea of what they mean. Do you ask if they really mean that persons are living in human form there? They talk about bodies there as indescribable bodies. Yet they sing:—

> "Come, let us join our cheerful songs
> With angels round the throne;
> Ten thousand thousand are their tongues,
> But all their joys are one."

This is a sublime song, in which every heart joins. The Church rings with it, and feels delighted with the idea of joining this glorious throng. But when many do so, they forget what their doctrine states; there has been no judgment; they have no bodies; and they are not to go to heaven at all till many thousands of years to come! We do not say, as our brother says in his sermon, that after the resurrection "the vaulted roofs" shall "echo back their shouts of triumph." I tell him they already echo with sounds of triumph. John heard them more than seventeen hundred years ago; when he saw the ten thousand times ten thousand that had come out of every nation and kindred and tongue. He says he heard them, and the glorious arches of eternity rang with: "Blessing, and glory, and wisdom, and thanksgiving, and honour, and power, and might be unto our God for ever and ever." And when we can join that company, heaven will ring with our voices too, and we shall not have to wait for any long indefinite period for that time. Oh! no. Why the poet Pope gave us a far more beautiful account than this, and what every heart feels to be the true one, the Scriptural one, when describing the dying man, he says:—

Lend, lend your wings! I mount! I fly!
O Grave! where is thy victory?
O Death! where is thy sting?"

That is the resurrection. Then is the real judgment. That is the entrance into eternity. This is what we preach, and what you believe, when you are under the influence of the love of the truth from the Scriptures, and not under the influence of the old announcements from the dark ages. Well, then, I say, do not think of this indefinite period, of a deferred entrance into life. The soul is the real man; let that be in the image of Jesus, and you will find that the eternal world is a real world—all below is shadow, all beyond is substance.

But we have said that there is not only a particular judgment which each person undergoes immediately after death on his entering into the eternal world, and which determines him to where he is suited for; but there is also, in the sacred Scriptures, not unfrequently mentioned a general judgment, and several such judgments. These likewise take place in the spirit-world, not in the world of nature. Here is the world of final preparation. The world of judgment is the world into which we enter. "It is appointed unto men once to die, but after this the judgment"—Heb. ix. 27. This is a doctrine which requires a little consideration, for it is a comprehensive one; but, owing to men having very much neglected the spirit and spiritual things, they have overlooked it. They have overlooked the teaching respecting the spirit-world, even when reading it in the sacred Scriptures. They have thought only according to the letter, but not according to the spirit: since the sun had gone down over the prophets, they have almost forgotten everything about the real nature of the spirit and the spirit-world. The spirit-world was well known in the early days of Christianity. Churches go on, as it were, in cycles; they have their beginning in which all is love and zeal and light. In the Jewish Church, when it commenced under the leading of the Patriarchs and Moses, while the people were animated by gratitude to God who had effectually redeemed them from slavery, and chosen them to be His people, they took the commandments of God and loved and obeyed them; but after a while, a different spirit set in, and, ultimately, darkness, folly, and night. And so it has been in relation to every Church. There has been a cycle—a beginning, a noon, an evening, and a night. This is frequently shown in the Scriptures. Under the name of "a new heaven and a new earth," a new Church is described. These terms mean a new dispensation, and when a former Church has gone on till men have corrupted it, made it of none effect by their tradition, it becomes like a broken-down, worn-out world. The old world, as it were, becomes ready to be destroyed—God, in some form, visits it—proclaims that its end is come—passes judgment upon it, and begins a new one.

Now this was pre-eminently done when our Lord and Saviour descended upon earth. Persons have been led—some by not thinking much about religion, and others by thinking only about one point in religion—a most important point, it is true, but one that has been magnified often to the exclusion of everything else,—I mean the death of the Lord Jesus Christ,—a most important portion of the Gospel, but one which ought not to exclude His life—nor the other grand things that are unfolded in the Sacred Scriptures. When the Apostle Paul said he was "determined not to know anything among men, save Jesus Christ, and Him crucified," he did not mean that Christians were not to think of anything else, but they were not to think of anything to the exclusion of that. There were men who came early into the church, and who denied God had appeared in the Church or come in the flesh at all. Some said He was not crucified at all, that Judas Iscariot was crucified in His stead. Some said His body was not a real body, but a phantasm. When the apostle insisted that Christ crucified was to be believed, it was not to be believed to the exclusion of his words and deeds, but to the exclusion of these fantastic dreams. Unhappily too many Christians at the present day have revived the notion of thinking so much about Christ's death, that they have not thought much about Christ's life, and very little about their own. He died that we might live; not that we might suppose we had nothing to do. A good old lady told me after the second lecture which I delivered here, that I completely spoiled Christ's atonement by saying that men had to do something. When the atonement was over, she said all was over. Man had nothing to do. She had thought only of God's being "in Christ, reconciling the world unto Himself," but not of the latter part—"Be ye reconciled to God." We must always avoid this error; we must get life from Christ to live ourselves; we must get power from Christ to conquer our sins; we must not take one precept of the Gospel and make it so large as to exclude all the rest; we must endeavour to have the whole counsel of God—death and life—Christ and man—God operating and man co-operating; and in this way endeavour to make our life Christ-like, and when we are made Christ-like He will take us to Himself. "Where I am, there shall also my servant be." But notwithstanding what the Lord Jesus has done, the man that does not enter into the spirit of heaven cannot go there. If he were let into heaven he would not be happy. He would be like a fish out of water,—a wolf being let into a fold of lambs;—he would be a vulture taken into a dove-cot. We must be angel-minded, or else we shall not be able to bear the very atmosphere of heaven. You will remember what Christ says about him who came in amongst the guests, and had not on a wedding garment: "Friend, how camest thou in hither, not having a wedding garment? And he was speechless."—Matt. xxii. 12. He had got truth and knowledge, but he had not married it to love or goodness; his garment was not a wedding garment, and he could not speak there—he was speechless;, what he had to utter could not be sounded in that holy region, and he had to go, bound hand and foot, into " outer darkness." Let us bear that well in mind.

Well, then, I was mentioning that Churches are spoken of as to their formation, under the name of new heavens and a new earth. Each has its beginning, its middle-period, and at length comes to its end. Now, after a Church has been corrupted, and then proceeds to corrupt the world and the ways of God for a considerable time, it becomes rather a school of error and mischief than of truth. Such the Church became in the days of Constantine. The Christian religion has been long supposed to have received a crown of glory then, because the Emperor had, after a certain fashion, embraced Christianity. A strange fashion it was, and a strange man he was; but still, because such a person had laid hold of Christianity, one who could make its ministers into "Right reverend Fathers in God," and give very ostentatious names and great power, it was supposed that the Church was going on gloriously, although at that very time it was fast losing its first love. The ministers were becoming men of pelf instead of piety; men to care about the fleece and not the flock; men who not only burned with hatred and revenge against each other, but absolutely contrived against the lives of each other. You will find, if you read the Church histories of that period, that under the influence of their dissensions and divisions they contrived against each other's lives. On one occasion, it is said that eighty ecclesiastics in returning from a council were sent to the bottom of the sea by the vessel being purposely set on fire by order, and the sailors leaving them to perish. This was the beginning of the persecution of each other, the quarrellings, the slaughterings, the councils, the creed-makings, the corruptions, which showed they had lost their love of Christianity for the love of themselves. Religion had perished, and now their chief objects were their dignities—their pelf—their power; they continually endeavoured to lord it over God's heritage. And whenever a man gets into that lordly self-seeking spirit, he is on the high-road to twist religion to make it suit himself—not to regard religion as that which is to make him like the meek and lowly

Jesus. And from the men of these times came the corruption of Christianity. Just as from the Jewish Pharisees and Sadducees came the corruption of Judaism. Judaism came into such darkness, that prophet after prophet had in vain exhorted them to repent—to come to the light, to serve God in spirit and in truth, still they persevered and sunk lower into sin and darkness until at length the Lord Jesus Christ came into the world to pass judgment upon them, and said, "It is finished—God has done with you for a Church—'It is finished'—it is the end of your world—it is the last day of your Church—it is time for you altogether to be swept away from pretending to be a Church in the Divine sight. A new one must begin from new principles—those that I bring into the world—which make the spirit of heaven to appear once more—the spirit of humility, of love, of following the light, of doing good, of serving others."

This is the new spirit out of which to form a new heaven and a new earth—such as St. Paul spoke of—" If any man be in Christ, he is a new creature: old things are passed away; behold, all things are become new." Now, not only does God proclaim in the world that "all things are become new," but He does judgment also in the spirit world. I have before said, when a Church begins to pervert its doctrines, to make everything dark and false, to suit everything to themselves—"like priest, like people "—darkness spreads over the mind—wicked principles spread over the life—men may call themselves Christians, but they are baptized infidels. They may talk about Christ in the spirit of that ruthless fiend of a man who, when heading an army of men called Christians, also in the war of the Albigenses in France, I mean the Abbot of Citeaux, at the town of Beziers, where there were fifty thousand people, men, women, and children; and when he had got possession of it, and was asked how were they to distinguish the faithful from the heretics—the early Protestants at that time, who gave their protests against priestly power and domination, his answer was, "Kill them all! God will know His own!" These men called themselves Christians, and were supposed to be led by a great Christian—he was a great ecclesiastic of the time. Such Christianity is the wickedest infidelity, it is the most ruthless spirit of hell, dignifying itself with the name of heaven. There is no real Church—no real Christianity in men and centuries of this class; and yet, if you look over all Christendom, such as it was through the middle ages, and down even to a hundred years ago all over Europe, and in this country, you will find it blind, ignorant, and persecuting on both sides. Roman Catholics were crushing Protestants, where they could, and Protestants were crushing Roman Catholics where they could. Both were fierce, stupid, and cruel. And yet there are foolish men who wish us to go back to the Church of those times. They speak ignorantly of such a Christianity as venerable and beautiful. We are very much better now. The world is advancing now to greater light and love. We are thinking now of alliances, not of divisions. Some can ally themselves now with others far more than they could even ten years ago. They can yet, perhaps, only ally themselves in certain points, but that is better than the old state. But what has made the turning point and change of spirit? THE JUDGMENT. When a religion has begun its downward course, growing darker and darker through centuries, even those who follow out conscientiously what they are taught, and think they are right in their religion, acquire error and faults which they can only be delivered from with difficulty. They think that when they persecute others at the command, perhaps, of their leaders, they are doing God's service. They die in these mistaken principles. Religion gets so mixed up in them, with dangerous errors inwoven into their souls by years of ardour, when they go into the other life, they cannot enter heaven. Nothing false can enter there. They were conscientious, and so are not at all fitted for the world of endless woe. I dare say there are many of my friends who are set against the idea of any intermediate place. We do not believe there is any such place as purgatory, but we do think there is a world of mind, called the intermediate state, a world of spirits, in which judgment takes place, and into which we go immediately after death, and with which our minds are connected now. Those who are thoroughly heavenly go at once to heaven; those who are thoroughly infernal go at once to hell; but those whose characters are so mixed, although their real motive is good, that they have been led by error into bad habits of various kinds, which yet they thought were right—these, in this intermediate place, have their errors removed. We do not think that heaven and hell are next-door neighbours. God does not teach that they are, in the parable of the rich man and Lazarus. You will remember it is said, "Between us and you there is a great gulf fixed," a great open place or state; heaven and hell are not just close together, "so that they which would pass from hence to you cannot, neither can they pass to us that would come from thence."—Luke xvi. 26. It is this intermediate state that is the place of judgment. During the many centuries in which a declining Church drags itself along, millions enter the world of spirits in a greatly imperfect state; some three thousand millions in a century. Upon a large portion of these multitudes, judgment takes place at the end of a Church. Now, my beloved friends, think whether you consider it rational that all persons, good and bad, should be taken to heaven to be judged; what shall the bad do there? or that the good and bad are taken to hell to be judged; it is not rational to think that the well-disposed go down there. If they are judged at all, there must be some place where they are judged. It is this intermediate world. Again, there are good people of every religion—good Roman Catholics—good Protestants—good Methodists—good Calvinists, and, no doubt, there are good Jews—good Mahommedans—and good Pagans, too: these persons have thought their views and sentiments right, and where are their errors to be corrected if there be not some middle region for instruction and judgment. We are told that nothing "which defileth, neither whatsoever worketh abomination, or maketh a lie," can go to heaven. But you do not think that real, sincere, good persons who only were attached to their religion—though it be Mahommedan—because they believed it to be God's religion—you do not think God will send them to hell? and they will not take Mahommedanism with them to heaven. Then what is to be done? There is this intermediate place where the angels instruct them in what is right, and remove these wrong notions from their minds. And that takes place which our Lord Jesus Christ speaks of, when He says, "For unto every one that hath, shall be given, and he shall have abundance; but from him that hath not shall be taken away even that which he hath." That is to say, a person who had the real spirit of heavenly goodness—loving the Lord, and desiring to obey His will—he has the root of the matter, but he has got a false creed; well, "unto every one that hath shall be given," and he will have all his difficulties explained, all his views set right; and "from him that hath not," who only seems to be good, all will be stripped off, so that he will have his naked soul, whatever it may be, exposed to men and angels, and he will go to his own: "For from him that hath not shall be taken away, even that which he hath."

Well, now, this is the place of judgment, and when a Church has been in a corrupt state for a considerable time, vast numbers congregate in this intermediate place, until the time when God puts an end to the false Church and begins another. He descends into that world with myriads of angels—effects judgment upon all who are there—unfolds all their states, which is called the opening of the books—consigns each to the place where he has to go; and this is the judgment that takes place at the end of a Church, not at the end of the outer world. In our English translation, we read of the end of the world; in the Greek, however, the New Testament phrase is the END OF THE AGE. Each dispensation is called an age. At the end of the Jewish age the Lord Jesus Christ effected a judgment, first in that world, and then planted His Church in this—made way for a new dispensation—that light and love might flow freely from Himself.

If you remember, you will find many instances in which this truth is taught in the Gospel. Jesus says, as you will read in John xii. 31, "Now is the judgment of this world; now shall the prince of this world be cast out." There was nothing outwardly going on of a very remarkable character, but He says, "Now shall the prince of this world be cast out;" He was clearing the inner world, and making way for the glorious influence of Divine light and love to flow out to the outer world, and this is the inner soul of a Church on the earth. Again, He says, "For judgment I am come into this world." Again, He says, as you will read in the sixteenth chapter of the same Gospel, "And when He is come, He will reprove the world of sin, and of righteousness, and of judgment; of judgment, because the prince of this world is judged." To these in this inner world the apostle alludes when he says, in 1 Peter iii. 18, 19, "Christ being put to death in the flesh, but quickened by the spirit: by which also He went and preached unto the spirits in prison." What were those spirits in prison, but the spirits that were in prison by false notions? Their souls were imprisoned by false ideas, until our Lord Jesus Christ went and set them free, and then took them to heaven with Him—leading captivity captive—the everlasting doors were opened to receive Him. How beautifully is this presented to us by St. Paul in Ephesians iv. 9, "Now that Christ ascended, what is it but that He also descended first into the lower parts of the earth?" "When He ascended up on high, He led captivity captive"—all spirits that remained in this intermediate region were freed from their captivity—all mistakes and wrongs taken away—the books were opened—the inward souls of men were brought out as to what they really were, and then the Lord "ascended up far above all heavens"—the everlasting doors were opened to receive Him, and He took all that were inwardly prepared with Him into their glorious homes, to form a new heaven, and from that a new earth among men. At the end of every Church this sublime proceeding takes place, and this is a general judgment, as awful and wonderful as it has commonly been thought, only it takes place in the spirit-world, and not in the world of nature. It takes place unseen to men, but revealed to them by the Lord—either by His own mouth, or by some other mouth commissioned by Him.

This work is very grandly spoken of by John the Baptist when our Lord is about to enter upon it. He said, "He it is, who coming after me, is preferred before me, whose shoe's latchet I am not worthy to unloose," but who "shall baptize you with the Holy Ghost and with fire; whose fan is in His hand, and He will throughly purge His floor."—Matt. iii. 11, 12. The floor is the barnfloor where the wheat is taken after it has been cut down in the fields. There it has to be threshed—there the chaff has to be stripped off and removed from the wheat—"He will throughly purge His floor and gather His wheat into the garner; but He will burn up the chaff with unquenchable fire." When, therefore, you read of a grand judgment in the Scriptures, it is the judgment in the spirit-world, at the end of a Church, that is meant. By clearing this world, God provides that the souls of men on earth shall be free for better things. The dark weight of folly and falsehood that has been hanging about men's souls is removed; for men on earth are in hidden connection with spirits—with spirits in the inner world. When things are rectified there, new light and love, with new freedom, flow down here—a new Church is formed —all things on earth become new. This was to be done at the end of the first Christian Church; and we believe it has been done, and that because it has been done we are living now in what every one feels to be A NEW AGE. There are new impulses in science, in reason, and religion. Everything is acquiring a new character. The great bulk of men are unable to tell how it is that everything now is progressing. We say, "Every good gift and every perfect gift is from above, and cometh down from the Father of lights" (James i. 17); it is because the old dispensation has come to its end and a new one has begun. A new and more generous spirit is permeating every sect—it is permeating every denomination—it is stirring the whole world. Protestants are not what they were some years ago: they are advancing. This man has got a new belief on one subject, that on another; one-half of every congregation does not believe much of what their creeds state. "We do not believe in that old Athanasian Creed," they say, "that is all nonsense." Not only is it so, but in Roman Catholic countries precisely the same advance is going on. In Roman Catholic lands I have met with men as liberal as the most liberal Protestants—quite a new thing in such latitudes. Everywhere you find these men advancing: getting more generous, more noble, more attractive, more Godlike, and more Christlike. The same spirit is pervading Mahommedan countries. The Sultan has proclaimed that every Christian shall be free—that the Bible shall be free in his land—that every man has a right to these blessings if he desire them. Nay, even that old stereotyped empire of China is being broken up too, so that God is making way for truth on every hand. He is teaching men everywhere to spread knowledge, to educate, to print, so as to turn out the materials of learning for every man, woman, and child, so that the knowledge of the Lord and the will of the Lord may be realized in this world of ours everywhere, not in one little sect, not in one small part of the earth, but all over the wide world. It may be that our country is to go first, and I believe that it is to lead the van in this glorious march. Ours is a land of freedom, the country of the Bible: I believe it is to be the leader in this—that it is to impress every land—it is to tell the whole families of the earth of the Divine impulse that is coming from on high—the impulse which fulfils the promise of Heaven, and says, "Behold, I make all things new." Prophecy has always said that this was to take place at some time. A person may say, "I believe in nothing new in religion—I do not admire anything new in the Church; I should never believe it, although God says 'I make all things new.'" Then you are a very foolish person for your pains. He declares that this time is to come, and now every one may see it is coming, and coming on in mighty strides. It is coming in science and arts, in kindness and benevolence, and who shall say it shall not come also in religion? Who is there that does not, in his own quiet thought, own that there are a thousand things he cannot understand, and does not long for a new light? Who is there that can look around and say, "Here are Christians up to the perfect mark; they cannot be mended at all?" Christians have been for some time improving, it is true, but they are very far from being what we all feel they ought to be. While God is making every other thing new, let us pray that we also may be made new—less sectarian, more united—less selfish, more Christian—less peevish, more angel-minded—less persecuting, more generous, kind, and good; realizing what the angels sung—"I heard the seventh angel sound, and there were great voices in heaven, saying, The kingdoms of this world are become the kingdoms of our Lord and of His Christ, and He shall reign for ever and ever."—Rev. xi. 15.

Oh! let us help to hasten on this glorious kingdom, and you who have a higher and holier view of our Lord and His Christ, or of Him who is both Lord and Christ, pray that He may practically reign for ever. Let us pray that He may reign over our thoughts—reign over our hearts—reign over our works—reign over our politics—reign over our homes—reign over our lives—reign over our deaths. "Come, Lord Jesus—come quickly!"

THE DISCUSSION.

Rev. J. Wilkins: In reference to the sermon just published, and to which some allusion has been made, I have only to state that I am responsible for all its faults; and as every person will have the opportunity of reading it for himself, I am perfectly satisfied that the decision will be in favour of the Word of God, and in favour, I believe, of the commonly received opinion in reference to the resurrection. Leaving that point, and coming to the lecture this evening, I have no desire to enter into any discussion upon it here, but I will undertake to do as I did last week (God willing); I will thoroughly consider the subject, and bring it before the public on Sunday evening. For if we discuss a point in public, it is very often that much is forgotten on both sides which might have been advanced. It is much better to bring the matter before the public in a more convenient way. There is just one point, however, and that is in reference to that intermediate state that we have been hearing of this evening. The Word of God tells us, "If ye believe not that I am He, ye shall die in your sins." Now, we have heard this evening, that if a man professes to love God—if the religion which he has received be false, and he is sincere in that religion, it is put right for him after he has departed from this life. Now, that is quite contrary to the Word of God, in my opinion. We will suppose the case of a Jew; he does not believe in Jesus Christ, and he dies in his sins, —" As the tree falls, so it must lie,"—and then he comes to the judgment in his sins. I should like you to give us a little light upon the subject. Is he to enter into everlasting rest, when he rejects the only Saviour, which is the Lord Jesus Christ?

Dr. BAYLEY: A very interesting question it is; and our friend will see that matters of this kind may be discussed in the calmest spirit. While he addressed us on this occasion no one has felt the least unpleasantness from his remarks. I am equally pleased with the question and the manner in which he has put it. Our view of the subject is this, Jesus Christ is the only God of heaven and earth, "in whom dwells all the fulness of the Godhead bodily." Every person that believes in a God of goodness and truth, although various men may call Him by various names, they really believe in Jesus Christ as the name above every name. Mahommedans call Him "Allah," which is in fact only the Hebrew name for God, as rendered into Arabic. The Hebrew name is "El," not God, as we have it. Inasmuch as Jesus Christ is really the God of heaven and earth, although the Mussulman does not know it; if he really believes in God he believes in the Lord Jesus Christ. Belief, of course, is meant as a living principle of action. When then a person believes, not simply as a speculation, but believes so as to carry out the will of God, he believes in the Lord, the only wise God, our Saviour. St. Peter himself said long ago, "In every nation he that feareth God, and worketh righteousness, is accepted of Him." The name of "Jesus" was not then known in every nation. There is not a quarter of the people of the earth now that knows the sound of the name of Jesus, or ever heard of the Gospel. Can we suppose that the God of love will send all these people to hell when they have never had a chance of hearing or reading the Gospel, or the word which we call the name of the Lord Jesus Christ? (Applause, and cries of "No.") This same blessed Saviour says, "And other sheep I have, which are not of this fold; them also I must bring, and they shall hear my voice; and there shall be one fold and one shepherd." He, therefore, in our estimation, who really believes in God, and shows he believes the truth, by working it out as he understands it, will hear all the truth he could not learn here about Jesus, when he goes into the other life. He will be of that "one fold," he will worship then that "one shepherd." That is our view.

Q. Did not the Jew that rejected the Lord Jesus Christ, did he not professedly believe in the God of heaven?

Dr. BAYLEY: The question, in our idea, is not what is professedly believed. Those with full knowledge who rejected the Saviour did not really believe. No man really believes in God, but he who works out God's will, and comes gladly to the truth. Our Lord Jesus Christ himself says that the

Jew who really did the will of God according to the teaching of Moses, would come to Him. Many did not really believe, and therefore their profession was worthless.

Q. If there is to be one fold, and one shepherd, how can those persons who never heard of Christ be saved?—how can Christ be a shepherd to them if they have never heard of Him? The Apostle in preaching, says, "There is no other name under Heaven, given among men, whereby we must be saved, but the name of Jesus Christ." If the name of Jesus Christ is not heard of, how can they believe in Him of whom they have not heard? "Faith cometh by hearing, and hearing by the Word of God." There must be a hearing of the name of Jesus, or there can be no salvation at all.

Dr. BAYLEY: Much more proper to ask, How can they be condemned for not believing in a name which they have never heard? In our estimation the word "name" does not simply signify a certain expression, it signifies the nature of a person. Jesus Christ says of "Him that overcometh, I will write upon him my new name." He does not mean that He will write the name Jesus on his forehead, but He wil. put His new nature—His new character upon him. By the name of Jesus is meant the nature of God manifest to men. That was His real character; we conceive that the real nature of God, as manifest to men, and impressing His will upon them, that is what is implied by the name of Jesus. You know that even in the Greek, the name is not the same as we have it in English. It does not mean that a certain word is to be heard; but that a nature should be felt which is to rule the hearts and minds of men: if that be lovingly carried out, we conceive it is then the name of Jesus written upon man. And thus, wherever that nature constitutes the root of the matter in them, they will take in the rest of heavenly truth when they have the opportunity, like a sponge takes water.

Q. Where is the necessity of preaching the Gospel if it is not true that the Gospel should be the means of salvation?

Dr. BAYLEY: The Gospel is a sacred truth, higher and

nobler than aught else, and the first grand thing in that truth is, as the Apostle says, faith, "for he that cometh to God must believe that He is, and that He is a rewarder of them that diligently seek Him." When a person has really this essential faith in God, and then comes to know that God is the Lord Jesus Christ, he has the Gospel. Those who have not the advantage of the Gospel in this world, but have the desire to live and follow out truth, will have the advantage of it in the eternal world. "Unto him that hath shall be given, and he shall have abundance." Shall we think of our God as unfeeling, instead of as a God whose "tender mercies are over all His works," as a God who never gives people the opportunity of being saved, and then damns them for ignorance—who lets the heathen go on (even now there is not a quarter of the human race that have heard of the Gospel) without knowing Him, and then torments them for ever for not believing what they could not know—this would be to us such a dreadful idea that we dare never attribute it to the God of love and mercy. (Loud cheers.)

Q. I think that the audience will feel with myself that one point Dr. Bayley has not answered, and I know he will be very pleased to make a reply. That is in reference to the Jew. You were talking about a man being sincere and going to heaven. Now, I believe that I can find hundreds of Jews who sincerely believe the Old Testament, but who sincerely believe that Jesus Christ was not the Messiah, and therefore they certainly reject Him; and believing not on Him, yet would they die innocent? You told us just now in your lecture, that however erroneous he may be, if he is sincere, all will be put right in the next world.

Dr. BAYLEY: I do not see the difficulty that I should attend to. The Jew who sincerely rejects, who, for instance, from education—from a variety of circumstances, is taught to reject, is not to blame. Christians have looked upon the Jews as the complete scapegoats of the human race—have regarded them with hateful feelings—have persecuted them—have shown their religion—if that was the religion of Jesus Christ—have shown it to them under the most odious and hateful forms. Now, is it to be wondered at that those who had been in the habit of seeing Christians ill treat them and their fathers, should not be very willing to hear what they had got to say about religion? It is the blame of Christians rather than of Jews that so little way has been made with really good Jews. I have been on the Continent and seen places distinguished as the scenes where Jews used to be persecuted. The Jews, from the bad treatment they have received, have been, as it were, divided by thousands of miles from Christians. A genuine Jew—one who has believed in the God of his fathers, has believed in Jehovah—has obeyed the will of Jehovah. Now our doctrine is, that Jehovah came in the flesh; so that he has really been to the best of his knowledge loving the very same person that we call Jesus Christ; and hence he has been in connection with the source of salvation. Jesus Christ says, "I am He who is, and who was—that very same Being—and who is to come,"—though He has been known before under another name, Jehovah, as the Lord Jesus Christ our Saviour, He is still the one God.

Q. But if the Jew rejected the visible presence of Christ when on earth, did he not reject Christ?

A. My dear friend, that can have nothing to do with the Jew now. The person who saw Christ in His real character when He was on earth, as " God manifest in the flesh," but who nevertheless rejected Him, certainly would be in a very different state from one who had never heard of His name or character. To reject Him then would be because he had a sinful hatred of all truth and goodness.

Q. But if the Jew altogether rejected Him?

A. Jesus Christ says, " Believe me that I am in the Father, and the Father in me; or else believe me for the very works' sake." He did the works that none but "God manifest in the flesh" could do; and the Jew that saw these works and still from interior opposition denied them, must have been in hatred against all that was good and true—he was not the person that we suppose, with real good intents and hopes and purposes.

Q. Just look at what Paul says of himself: "An Hebrew of the Hebrews; as touching the law, a Pharisee; touching the righteousness which is in the law, blameless." Do we suppose that this was an isolated character?

A. Saul of Tarsus was saved as soon as he had knowledge of Christ. Christ removed the ignorance that he was labouring under, and he came really into the fold of Christ.

Q. You would suppose that there were only very few that were sincere among all the Jews; they did not believe the things professed?

A. They had made the commandment of God of none effect by their own tradition. The Jews then were a church in ruins. At such times there is great profession, but little practice. Profession without practice is not faith. The vast majority of the Jews were faithless and dark, and loved darkness rather than light, because their deeds were evil. The Lord Jesus said, "This is the CONDEMNATION, that light is come into the world, and men loved darkness rather than light because their deeds were evil."—John iii. 19. Men are not condemned for not receiving light which has never visited them. But when light comes, and from evil is rejected, then is SIN and then is CONDEMNATION. Only a few among the Jews received the Saviour; the great majority were obstinate in wickedness, and from wickedness rejected Him who would have saved them. To them the Saviour said, "If ye believe not that I am He, ye shall die in your sins." But this is a very different case from that of a person NOW: who has taken his impressions of Christianity, and of its Divine Human Head, the Saviour, not from Himself, but from teachers prejudiced by ill-treatment, or from the conduct of those who are Christians only in name. Such a Jew may reject Christianity, and yet may inwardly be the very person who would receive it when he understood its real character and worth. Such a person, inwardly good, will have an opportunity provided for him by that merciful

Providence who notices and numbers the hairs of our heads and the fall of a sparrow. And if there are those who, as Tennyson says,

> " Perplext in faith, but pure in deeds
> At last who beat their music out.
> There lives more faith in honest doubt
> Believe me, than in half the creeds,—"

we cannot condemn such. We are sure Divine mercy will save all who are salvable. None will perish for want of knowledge and opportunity. And as many have not the opportunity, nor the true knowledge of right in this world, there must be another in which these will be given. The saying of Ecclesiastes is not opposed to this doctrine, when rightly understood. "If the tree fall toward the south, or toward the north, in the place where the tree falleth there it shall lie."—xi. 3. For this only teaches that the direction and interior place of a person is fixed at death; and this is fixed by the state of the heart, not by doctrine, profession, knowledge, or community. "The Lord looketh upon the heart."—1 Sam. xvi. 7. The height of a tree is determined when it falls, but it has much shaping to undergo before it becomes a towering mast, or an article of furniture. So the inner life of man is fixed at death, as to his ruling love being good or evil; but as to his state of knowledge, belief, association, or mistakes in conduct, arising from ignorance or false teaching, these will be often greatly changed. And let us adore the Divine goodness that it is so. "In our Father's house there are many mansions." And the good of all ages, of all nations, of all climes, and of all creeds, will find unending peace in those celestial homes best adapted for them. Socrates, with his virtuous sagacity; Plato, with his profound philosophic insight; Cicero, with his burning eloquence, replete with justice and wisdom; Augustine, with his adoring gaze and sublime conceptions; Bernard, with the sacred unction of glowing earnest sanctity; Luther, with his heartfelt honest boldness for truth, and horror of superstitions and deceits; Fenelon, with his saintly sweetness and holy meekness; Wesley, with his untiring zeal; Taylor, Ken, Tillotson, Heber, models of hallowed piety and sacred wisdom; Swedenborg, with his pure, gigantic, systematic, God-given genius, wise and wonderful recognition of Divine love and wisdom and self-repudiation of heart,—these and myriads out of all nations, kindreds, and tongues, with their talents all sanctified and expanded, all who were sheep of the Divine pasture of truth here, so far as they knew it, who followed the voice of the Great Shepherd, when they heard it, these will all be arranged and harmonized in the communions of eternity, and be led by the adorable Lamb to the living waters of ever increasing wisdom to all eternity.

THE SIXTH LECTURE.

THE SECOND COMING OF THE LORD.

"Immediately after the tribulation of those days shall the sun be darkened, and the moon shall not give her light, and the stars shall fall from heaven, and the powers of the heavens shall be shaken: and then shall appear the sign of the Son of man in heaven: and then shall all the tribes of the earth mourn, and they shall see the Son of man coming in the clouds of heaven with power and great glory."—*Matt.* xxiv. 29, 30.

"And when He was demanded of the Pharisees, when the kingdom of God should come, He answered them and said, The kingdom of God cometh not with observation."—*Luke* xvii. 20.

PRAYER BEFORE THE LECTURE.

O LORD JESUS, King of kings and Lord of lords, Father, Son, and Holy Spirit, God over all, blessed for ever, we come to Thee. We bless Thy holy name for the promise that the time shall come, in which Thou wilt show us plainly of the Father; and we pray for its fulfilment. We bless Thy holy name for the assurance that the knowledge of Thee shall cover the earth as the waters cover the sea, and none shall hurt nor destroy in all Thy holy mountain. Hasten, adorable Saviour, this happy period. Spread, we beseech Thee, the desire to know Thee, to believe in Thee, and to love Thee. Destroy in us, Thy servants, every obstacle to Thy holy government. May Thy kingdom come, and Thy will be done on earth, as it is done in heaven. May Thy Divine government be accepted over the earth and continue for ever and ever. These mercies we ask in Thine own blessed name, Lord Jesus, and for Thy goodness' sake. Amen.

LECTURE.

THE question for us to dwell upon to-night is, Will the coming of the Lord Jesus Christ a second time be a coming in person or in spirit? Is it to be an outward display in the sky, and an alteration in the material universe, or is it to be the descent of new principles from the Lord, forming human souls on earth to be an image below of His glorious kingdom in heaven? To these questions we reply, Undoubtedly it is to be a coming in spirit and not in person; NOT BY OUTWARD SHOW OR OBSERVATION.

We would beg of you to bear in mind this fact, that all the teaching which we esteem to be scriptural and harmonious with the whole counsel of God, must come up to the threefold test of which I spoke last evening; namely, it must be rational, it must be in harmony with science, it must be scriptural. In relation to doctrines also, we require that they should be taught in the very language of the sacred Scriptures; not simply that the ideas should be in harmony with the spirit of the Bible, but the foundation principles should be absolutely expressed in the very language of the Bible. The very language of the Bible in answer to this question you will find in our second text, Luke xvii. 20, 21. The Pharisees and scribes questioned Jesus about the coming of the kingdom of God, and He said, "The kingdom of God cometh not with observation: neither shall they say, Lo here! or, lo there! for, behold, the kingdom of God is WITHIN YOU."

Now, that is precisely what we teach upon the subject; everything else comes in the way of illustration. The very letter of the Scripture teaches the true doctrine. It is so with every doctrine we teach. As a doctrine we not only know that it is in harmony with the whole Scriptures, but it is such as to be stated in the very language of the Scriptures—it is "Thus saith the Lord." It is not so with what may be called the old doctrines of Christendom; not one of them can be stated in the very language of the sacred Scriptures. They are supposed to be inferred—supposed to be proveable by something else that is stated, but they are nowhere said in so many words. To illustrate this, begin with the doctrine of the Godhead. This says, there are three Divine persons in God, and these three form one God. You cannot find this, however, stated anywhere in the Bible; not even two Divine persons are mentioned there. It is not to be found from Genesis to Revelation. I can find plenty of statements to the opposite. God is ONE, is the grand doctrinal note. And so it is with every one of the peculiar doctrines which have been very commonly supposed to be the doctrines of true religion. Not one of them can be stated in the exact and precise language of the Bible. If I ask a man to bring me a passage of Scripture that says the natural body shall rise again—that the material body shall rise again—that flesh and blood shall rise again, or anything which specifically states what he means upon that subject in the very words of the Bible, he cannot find it in the whole of the Scriptures. The dead shall rise is to be found there; but how, or in what body shall they come? That is the particular inquiry—How they are to rise, and when? Ask me for a passage that says flesh and blood shall not rise, and I give you one in a moment, "Flesh and blood cannot inherit the kingdom of God; neither doth corruption inherit incorruption." "The body thou sowest is NOT the body that shall be." I can give you half a dozen if you like, to state in scriptural expression our view upon the subject. And now upon the subject of this lecture, the question is, whether the second coming of the Lord is to be by outward show—by a visible appearance in the sky—or whether it is by an inward change, to take place by new principles being given: and here is the Word of the Lord, "The kingdom of God cometh NOT BY OUTWARD OBSERVATION." Not. It is easy and simple; short and to the point. Men shall not say, "Lo here! or, lo there!" is it to come in the eastern sky, or the western sky? "FOR THE KINGDOM OF GOD IS WITHIN YOU."

Well now just think for a moment of this beautiful and scriptural statement as to the "how." It is not as to the fact whether the Lord will come and form a new kingdom or not, BUT HOW IT IS TO BE DONE? Just think of it—consider whether this scriptural statement—that it is not by outward show—is not as rational as it is scriptural? Have not men been going on for hundreds of years thinking that they could make themselves happy by outward show?—some by an outward show in religion—some by an outward show in irreligion—one man by the terrible ambition of royal, imperial, or priestly rule; another man by thinking that he should be thoroughly happy if he only managed to get a thousand pounds, or a house of a certain size, or in some way be blest by external grandeur; and has there ever been a man made happy by that means? Is it not evident to a thoughtful mind that this world—this glorious universe of our God—this grand canopy on high, and this beautifully carpeted earth in which we live—is the sublime creation of infinite Love and Wisdom; and what is needed to make this world a paradise, but that men should become outwardly and inwardly permeated by the spirit of God, and as obedient to His will as the outward world is? What is it that makes the world unhappy? False and wicked principles. Take these away, and this world would then become—it is true in a lower degree, yet it would become for man—the outward kingdom of our God; this world would then become a world of preliminary and preparatory happiness; a nursery for heaven; a place of preparation where, as far as inward spiritual powers and beauties and blessings could be expressed by the body and in the body—we should have a heaven upon earth. There is nothing amiss with the world; there is nothing wrong with the sky; there is nothing wrong with God's part of creation; it is man's selfishness and sin that make the mischief. Let there be unfolded in the spirits of men, true, Godlike principles, not the revelation of Divine wisdom perverted—let it be seen what it is that makes heaven there, and insisted upon that the same principles must be acted upon here, and you then have the powers of heaven brought down upon earth; you have that fulfilled which, probably, you have every one of you been praying for to-day and every day; for our blessed Lord taught us all to do it—"Thy kingdom come, Thy will be done, as in heaven, so upon the earth." That has not yet been the case. Not yet, even though prayed for so long. But surely it is to be. Surely all this teaching, and all this prayer, and all the promises of the sacred Scriptures are to be fulfilled some time or other. And may it not be that mistaken notions of religion have stood in the way of their being fulfilled hitherto—and that true ideas of religion will bring about the fulfilment that is wanted? It is rational to think so. Thus is it with an individual. "If any man is in Chris, the is a new creature. Old things have passed away, ALL THINGS HAVE BECOME NEW." Then it is within the experience of every person that it is an inward change which is wanted—a real inward change. Instead of self ruling in the soul, Christ ruling there; instead of fanciful and self-conceited notions being what we act upon, the holy principles that form the essence of all religion being what we shall act upon. "Thou shalt love the Lord thy God with all thy heart, and with all thy soul, and with all thy mind. This is the first and great commandment. And the second is like unto it, Thou shalt love thy neighbour as thyself. On these two commandments hang all the law and the prophets."

This view is rational then, as well as scriptural, and it is in harmony with science. Science says nothing about the Lord Jesus Christ coming in an outward way, and the world being destroyed, and the universe being made into an awful wreck. We invite especial attention to the language of our text. Every now and then persons rise up, who come with great zeal and energy, and declare that either in a few weeks, or a few years, this general wreck and conflagration are to take place; and they agitate the minds of simple and ignorant persons until these become frantic almost, and sometimes quite, with the idea that there is to be complete annihilation of the present universe—there is to be, an utter wreck of worlds and suns, and that this is to be the attendant of the second coming of our Lord Jesus Christ. And here, I may remark, such persons would select my first text as their peculiar authority for teaching this. There are a few texts which are commonly made use of, but none more striking than this, and for that reason I have selected it: and allow me to mention that with us it is the common practice to do so. We believe that the true mode by which Christians are to get at right views is not by shirking the views of other people, or shunning the texts that other people suppose their views are taught by, but looking them straight in the face, and making the entire Scripture harmonise together: and when you can not only see your own, but harmonise the others with it, there is tolerable reason to believe that you have got the right key to the whole. It is too often with religion as it was with the outer garment of the Saviour when He was crucified. The soldiers divided the garments amongst them. Too often it has happened that fighting Christians, those who have been earnest in dispute, have overlooked the spirit of real religion—each has taken his piece—each has kept his part of the garment. They have divided His garments amongst them. And, precisely in this way, the Bible has been taken piece-meal; each taking his bit, and scarcely ever looking at what appears to be of a somewhat opposite character. The safer principle is the other; take what seems to be contrary to your view, and examine that well, see what you can make of that. There is no real contrariety. But when a person takes his part of the letter of the Scriptures, abides in the letter, and pays no attention to the spirit or the grand entirety of Divine revelation, then comes error. "The words that I speak unto you," said the Lord Jesus, "they are spirit, and they are life." "The letter killeth," saith St Paul, "but the spirit giveth life."

Well, now, as to this first passage. It says that about the time when our Lord shall come, and previous to His coming, "the sun shall be darkened, and the moon shall not give her light, and the stars shall fall from heaven;" and the common notion has been that this is literally to happen. And while men had no true knowledge of the grandeur of the system of the universe—while they supposed that this world was not so large as it is, and that the sky was just a blue arch raised over the world, in which the stars as lamps were fixed, or they were glory-holes through which light gleamed from heaven which was just above it—while they had this kind of notion, the idea of the stars falling to the earth did not seem to them a very startling thing or an irrational one at all. But now it is known that our earth is not the centre of the universe, nor is it larger than all the rest of the universe put together, as it used to be thought. It is known that our earth is only a comparatively small portion of our own solar system—that our sun is as large as thirteen hundred thousand earths put together—that some of the planets in our solar system are many hundred times larger than our earth; and there are about ninety planets, greater or less, belonging to our solar system. It is known that our solar system all together, the sun and all his worlds if seen from another fixed star, another sun—all together would only seem like a point, like a star; the worlds would be hidden in the glorious beams of the sun, and seen from another star, the whole would only be as one star in the firmament. When it is seen that there are millions of such stars which are doubtless suns, and attended by their worlds revolving round them too, then "the heavens indeed declare the glory of God." This is not all; the most powerful telescopes discover to us small, dim bodies which have been called "nebulæ," because they have a cloudy look, even to telescopes of less power; these, more powerful telescopes discover that these small bodies that seemed not larger than the hand are also crowds of stars—other grand starry systems, and that these also, when they are seen to be stars, most probably with suns and worlds again, have other dim nebulæ unveiled. The most powerful telescopes discover other cloudy bodies behind these—other systems, other grand collections of suns and worlds. When, I say, we come to see how wondrously grand is this universe of our God—that some of these worlds, some of these suns even, are so far distant that light would take millions of years to come from them to us; what then are we to think of the idea of the stars falling down to the earth, when one of the secondary class, one that is only one of millions, is many hundred times larger than the earth! Why then surely science necessitates our thinking a little more about that subject, to see whether we have got the right system of interpretation or not. With our view, we shall easily perceive how beautifully the Divine sense coheres and comes out too. With the ordinary view, let a person just think that, first of all, as we said before, one star is far too large even to be received upon the earth. Let him imagine that the notion even of all the stars *falling* to the earth is unphilosophical, because the earth is suspended in space, and the stars are all around, so that a very large portion of them would have to rise to the earth instead of falling to it—others would have to approach on the same level: and these wonderful bodies, if they were to be making their way to the earth, millions of millions of miles before they got there, would all be wedged fast. Again, such is the power of gravitation that very, very long before these suns and worlds even came together, they would so powerfully attract our world as to rend it to atoms—there would be no world to come to—it would be all gone into ten thousand thousand thousand atomic forms.

A person may say, "I have nothing to do with that; I have to believe the Scriptures." The question is not respecting believing the Scriptures; the question is of understanding the Scriptures. And if you choose to abide by the letter, the "letter" that "killeth," instead of coming unto the "spirit" that "giveth life," rest assured you are not honouring God; you are merely yourself sticking to a piece of unreasonable nonsense, and dishonouring God who teaches you by science and by reason, and also by the express teaching which I have already quoted, that His kingdom does not come with OUTWARD SHOW. God teaches you to come from the letter, up to some higher signification; and if we are at all conversant with the sacred Scriptures, we shall have no difficulty in reading these glorious symbols.

God who made the spiritual, moral, and outward worlds, has made them all beautifully corresponding to one another. And one of the grandest of all sciences is the science of seeing the relation, the correspondence, that there is between outward things and inward things, between matter and spirit, between the outward universe of nature and the inward universe, the universe of mind.

Now it is according to this grand law that God speaks in the Bible; and you will find there that sun and moon and stars, that heaven and earth, are not used in the sense of the earthly and material objects which are understood when men are speaking about earthly things. But by the "sun" is meant the higher sun, the sun of the soul—God Himself; by the "moon" is meant a higher and nobler moon, that faith which reflects God's light upon the soul, as the moon reflects the light of the sun upon the earth; and that the "stars" are used as the symbols in the sacred Scriptures of all the lesser lights of heavenly knowledge, of the sciences of heavenly things given in the sacred Word, when understood—each one shining like a little star in the soul.

In this way the Church is like that glorious image given us in the beginning of the twelfth chapter of Revelation, where it is said by John, "And there appeared a great wonder in heaven; a woman clothed with the sun, and the moon under her feet, and upon her head a crown of twelve stars; and she travailed with a man-child." Every one will see how beautiful the image becomes when we bear in mind that the woman, or the Church—which is represented by a woman throughout the Bible—the Church is the Lamb's wife; she has the sun of God's love around her; she has the moon of faith for her support; she has the inward ornaments of all the knowledges of heavenly things shining about her head; she brings forth the true doctrine which forms men-children—those that are really men, God's men—those that really bring out all that is angelic and manly—those that rule everything within them in subordination and obedience to the Divine will—that rule all nations with a rod of iron.

I have said that the "sun" is the corresponding image to God Himself, especially His Divine love. And here perhaps one may ask, "Well, but where is there a text for that?" It is quite ready. You will find it in Psalm lxxxiv. 11, "For the Lord God is a sun and shield: the Lord will give grace and glory: no good thing will he withhold from them that walk uprightly." If you want another, look to Isaiah lx. 20, "Thy sun shall no more go down; neither shall thy moon withdraw itself (you have the moon as well there): for the Lord shall be thine everlasting light, and the days of thy mourning shall be ended." If you wish for further evidence, turn to Malachi iv. 2, "But unto you that fear my name shall the Sun of righteousness arise with healing in His wings."

How beautiful is the idea that the soul has its sun as well as the body; that there is a true light that enlightens every man that comes into the world—that same glorious Sun who, in the person of the Divine Saviour, came to reconcile the world unto Himself, and of whom John says, the Baptist was not the light; but Jesus was the light, "the true Light, which lighteth every man that cometh into the world."

Now this is the Sun with which the Scriptures have to do. It is our relationship to that Sun that is of the highest importance to all of us; and if we can open our souls to let that Sun shed its glorious light upon our hearts, we may then walk on, illuminated and blessed by its splendour, which will ever throw a light upon our path, and enable us to advance from light to light unto the perfect day.

In fact it is in this way alone that we can understand the Scriptures, either when they speak of a new heaven and earth being formed, or of the old one being broken down and dissolved.

Here allow me to direct your attention for a moment to some passages in the Scriptures to which men commonly appeal. They are not many in number; but they are some that, to people who do not think deeply, seem to say exactly what they imagine them to say—that the world is to be dissolved, and the heavens also, with great heat—at the same time, simply because they have not observed the scriptural mode of speaking. They take their notions to the Bible, and interpret the Bible according to them, instead of just taking their minds to the Bible, and letting it teach them. Now, if they had taken the other plan—read steadily the sacred pages—they would have found there that whenever God speaks of forming a new dispensation after the end of an old one, He calls it making a new heaven and a new earth; and when a religion becomes faded, perverted, and broken down, it is called the old heaven and earth being dissolved, and passing away. This is the mode in which God speaks throughout the Scriptures. In all these things we are most strikingly instructed in the sacred writings themselves. Take, for instance, as an evidence of the mode of forming a dispensation, Isaiah li. 16, "And I have put my words in thy mouth, and I have covered thee in the shadow of mine hand, that I may PLANT THE HEAVENS, AND LAY THE FOUNDATIONS OF THE EARTH, and say unto Zion, Thou art my people." Now here, you perceive, God speaks of planting the heavens, and laying the foundation of the earth. But every one will know that when He puts His words into the prophet's mouth, or when He puts His words into your mouth or mine, He does not then and thereby make the outward universe, which was made thousands and millions of years before. But yet this is called "planting the heavens and laying the foundation of the earth, and saying to Zion, Thou art my people." But what "heavens"? The heavens within—the heavens with which we have to do. What "earth"? The new earth of a new life and conduct—new institutions, to which the new heavens give rise—new practice, a new outside as well as a new inside. This is called the "planting of the heavens, and laying the foundations of the earth." Take, again, Isaiah lxv. 17, 18, and you will find, where the Lord is speaking of founding the Christian world, He says, "For, behold, I create new heavens and a new earth; and the former shall not be remembered, nor come into mind. But be ye glad and rejoice for ever in that which I create: for, behold, I create Jerusalem a rejoicing, and her people a joy." But if creating a new heaven and earth meant that He would do away with the natural universe and form a new natural universe, it would be no rejoicing for Jerusalem or her people either, for they would have to perish along with the rest of the earth. But, then, when we read the Scriptures attentively, we are at no loss to see what is meant is the removal of the old principles, which have formed a wretched state of society, and bringing forth new principles to form a new and holy and pure state of society. The "last days" and the "end of the world," do not mean the last days, or the end of the outward world; but the end of the former dispensation—the former Church, the former mode of thinking and acting. We are not only taught in the Scriptures that the earth will be dissolved, but you will find precisely the same language used concerning what it has been. In David's time the Jewish Church became corrupted. Saul, who ought to have been its great protector, became forgetful of his God—a breaker of all Divine ordinances—a conspirer against the truly good; and how is that described? Look at Psalm lxxv. 3, and there you will read, "The earth and all the inhabitants thereof are dissolved. I bear up the pillars of it"—not shall be dissolved at some future time, but *are*, are now dissolved. No one with common sense can suppose that the outward world in David's time was all dissolved and done away with; and that he, like another Atlas, was propping up the outward system of things.

But that is the way in which Divine revelation speaks. Because, as I said before, the earth with which it has to do is the moral earth, the spiritual earth, not the outward material world. The outer earth is all right. What we have to do is to receive God's principles into ourselves, and use God's Word aright. It is not any isolated state of things of which I am speaking, but it is interspersed throughout the Word of God. It is very often found to be the case, that when a person comes upon a new truth in science, he is astonished that he was so dull he never saw it before, when it has been lying under his nose all his life long, and when others see it they wonder that they never found it out. And so it is in religion. When you get a real new view— one that is an advance in Divine revelation, you wonder you never saw it before. So it is with this view; it is found interspersed through all the sacred pages, yet numbers read without perceiving it. Turn to Psalm lxxxii. 5, "They know not, neither will they understand; they walk on in darkness: all the FOUNDATIONS OF THE EARTH ARE OUT OF COURSE." Well now, no one surely can suppose that because the people would not understand, and would not know and act upon the principles of true heavenly light, the rocks went out of course: "the foundations of the earth are out of course." But the foundations of what earth? Why, the foundations of the moral earth—the foundations upon which all men must build if they would have a solid superstructure of holiness, wisdom, and true righteousness. The grand foundation is Jesus Christ and His Divine commandments—these form the foundations. But when men will not have them—when they love darkness rather than light—when they walk on in darkness, then these foundations get out of course. You will find it just the same in every one of the prophets, the same in the gospels, and in the epistles. We have the end of the world, or, as we have mentioned before, it ought to be translated, the end of the age—we have it in this very chapter, the twenty-fourth of Matthew, from which our text is taken. The Lord says, in answer to the inquiry of the disciples about the end of the age, called the end of the world, " But he that shall endure unto the end, the same shall be saved "—that the time shall come when "iniquity shall abound, and the love of many shall wax cold. But he that endures unto the end shall be saved." Well, but what will be meant by enduring to the end of the natural universe—living on unto the end of the world? Why, if none were to be saved but those who did so, then all those that have died up to this time must be lost; for the world has not ended yet. Jesus says, "He that endureth to the end;" that is to say, when religion is becoming perverted and cold; and although men may talk a great deal about faith then, it is faith in something of their own; it is not faith in what Jesus teaches and lays down; it is very often only the name of faith. When men talk about faith alone being saving, it is not the faith of Jesus Christ. There is no such thing with Him as faith alone. He does not recognise such a faith; His Apostles did not recognise it. If a person has nothing but faith, he has not faith; he has only fancy. He alone is saved by faith whose faith is full of love, and goes out into practice. It is never faith alone. " Though I have all faith," says St. Paul, " so that I could remove mountains, and have not charity, I am nothing." " Show me thy faith without thy works," says James, "show it me; let me look at it, and I will show thee my faith by my works." That alone is true faith. Tell me what a man does, and I shall know what he believes. He may talk about his faith from morning to night; if I see he is acting from a spirit of selfishness and injustice, he does not believe in Christ, he believes in himself—that is his faith, the other is a sham thing—one he talks about and keeps for show, and perhaps after deceiving others for a long time, he at last deceives himself, and supposes he believes what he talks about believing. He has got something that is not what the Lord Jesus recognises as faith. He said to the woman that loved Him, "Thy faith hath saved thee." When persons love Him, then their faith will act; for it is faith not alone, it is full of love. This is the only faith that Jesus Christ recognises as faith—that which the Apostle speaks of when he says, "For in Jesus Christ neither circumcision availeth anything, nor uncircumcision; but faith which worketh by love." That is saving faith.

Well, then, the Lord teaches that before His coming there would be a great lack of faith—that the sun would be darkened, and the stars should fall from heaven.

But, I have said, that the end of the world, the last day, and such-like expressions, refer to the end of a dispensation, not to any destruction of the material world, and that this is the meaning in the New Testament as well as in the Old. We will just examine it in the New Testament.

We have already said that our Lord's words would be unintelligible if we thought of the end of the world. But where a man is faithful, and stands by the truth and the love of Jesus Christ, and will not swerve from this—though he sees his neighbour getting rich by cheating, and his neighbour believes in cheating—he is a man who believes in Christ, believes in justice, believes in goodness, and clings firmly to these, not only in his prayers and on a Sunday, but in his practice and every day in the week, that man has real faith; he is enduring to the end, and he will be saved. The other man is getting lost in the wreck, and he will not be saved.

At the end of the Jewish system, which was called "the end of the world," or "the end of the age," and "the last days," you will find the use of the term ends of the world by the Apostle Paul in 1 Cor. x. 11, " Now all these things happened unto them for examples: and they are written for our admonition, upon whom the ends of the world are come." Not will come, but "are." Here we have the very expression itself: the Apostle says it was the end of the world. But of what world? Why, the Jewish world, the Jewish dispensation, which had altogether become corrupt and false. And the Lord Jesus Christ from His cross proclaimed it to be come to an end, "It is finished," and the veil of the temple was rent in twain—all over with that dispensation; there was the end of it. See also Heb. ix. 26.

You will find that in the Apostolic language the terms "last days" and "last time" very frequently occur. As for instance, the Apostles, when preaching on the Day of Pentecost, were charged with being drunk, and Peter stood up and said, "These are not drunken . . . But THIS IS THAT which was spoken by the prophet Joel, And it shall come to pass in the LAST DAYS, saith God, I will pour out of my spirit upon all flesh . . . And I will show wonders in heaven above, and signs in the earth beneath; blood, and fire, and vapour of smoke," and so on. Precisely a similar passage to what we have in our text, only that Joel had spoken of it hundreds of years before Christ came; and when Christ came and put an end to the Jewish Church, and commenced the Christian Church, what that prophet said, "was in these last days fulfilled." These were the last days of that dispensation, and the first days of a better and a higher. So, again, in the beginning of the Epistle to the Hebrews, Paul says, "God hath IN THESE LAST DAYS spoken unto us by His Son." Mind, in *these* last days. St. John says, "Little children, it is the last time;" and that was eighteen hundred years ago, but it was then the last time, the last days, the end of the world.

All these declarations were given then, and applicable even to that time, but, as we have said before, what was it that came to an end? It was the former dispensation, not the world. This was God's mode of teaching that the moral system had become corrupted, and was altogether nc longer carrying out God's will, and it was time for it to be done away with; and He did away with it. The new Christian Church is called a new heaven and a new earth. When it was said that this was to occur again, it is to teach us that the principles He gave to man in Christianity would again be corrupt—again would delusion come instead of faith—again would selfishness come instead of love—again would blindness come instead of the light of life; and therefore, Christ said that "the sun shall be darkened, and the moon shall not give her light, and the stars shall fall from heaven." And has it not been so? If the sun be, as we have said, the love of God shining upon the heart—the Sun of righteousness pouring out His Divine influences over the affections, has not that been darkened? We are now rising gradually from the depth of darkness into which men sunk—rising, and have been rising for a considerable time to somewhat better things; but even NOW every one knows we are nothing to boast of. God's love is darkened in too many hearts, even now. Why, is it not a common thing for persons to say to themselves, "Where is there a real Christian? I know plenty of professors, but where are those in whom the love of Christ is continually operating?" God be thanked, there are some few, here and there. But is it not the case that we in this land of enlightenment and Bibles—that even with us, every one feels that there is only here one and there one, and that to the vast mass the sun is still darkened? But how tremendous was that darkness when Christians, during the middle ages, were engaged in infernal hate—persecuting one another even to death: persecuting one another in almost every land! How terrible must have been the darkness that shut out the sun of heaven from the human spirit! "The moon," it is said, "shall not give her light; and the moon we have seen represents holy faith, not in some scheme of our own, but a faith in the living light that comes from Jesus Christ, and is reflected upon the soul when it is going on in the darkness of spiritual night. The soul has its nights as well as the body. There are times of glory and blessing in which the sun is felt to be shining; and there are times in which there are shade and night—we can hardly see light, look where we may. There are times of sorrow and distress. God leaves us to ourselves that we may see and know what we are. "Weeping may endure for a night," the Psalmist says, "but joy cometh in the morning." It would be entirely darkness but that faith, like a silvery moon, lends her light, and tells us to "hope—trust in God—fear not, I will be with thee—hope—night won't always last—be faithful, and in a little time a new morning will break over the spirit, and thou wilt come to a state of blessedness again." "Then shall we know, if we follow on to know the Lord." This is the moon shining over the soul. But when men have falsified religion—when their views have altogether become immersed in terrible colours—when they say that nobody can be saved only those who belong to their little clique—and there is no salvation for those out of their chapel or sect—the moon is being darkened, the highest and brightest and divinest blessings are being driven away from the soul. It is a God of love that gives men comfort. It is a God unchangeable, kind, and gentle—it is our holy Saviour breathing love; and when we are in the depths of sorrow, He stretches out His hands, and says, "Come unto me, all ye that labour and are heavy laden, and I will give you rest." But when the moon is darkened, it is a bad time with the soul. This is that which is meant, when it is said concerning this time of bitterness, "Woe unto them that are with child, and to them that give suck in those days." That is, woe to them that are trying earnestly to be born again—that are trying to have the new man of the heart born from God within them—woe to them; it is hard with them when false religion is prevailing, and true religion giving no light; it is hard for them when they are trying to become new men —and feed upon "the sincere milk of the Word,"—"woe to them that give suck in those days"—when the Bible is either closed through false interpretation, or not allowed to be in their hands at all; it is "woe to them that give suck in those days," almost all the milk is turned into poison. The stars fall from heaven.

We have said that the stars mean the lights of heavenly knowledge. Every verse of the Scriptures becomes a "star" when you understand it. It becomes like a beautiful little light that gives its ray in the right place and at the right time. That is the sort of star that St. Peter spoke of in his second epistle, first chapter, and nineteenth verse: "We have also a sure word of prophecy, whereunto ye do well that ye take heed, as unto a light that shineth in a dark place, until the day dawn, and the day star arise in your hearts." It is a star that rises in the heart; the same sort of star is meant by Jesus in Revelation ii. 28: "To him that overcometh, I will give the morning star." No one will suppose that He means, that to the man who overcomes in his spiritual conflict, He will give an earthly morning star, either Jupiter or Venus; no one will be so ridiculous as to think so. Oh, no; the star that Jesus gives is a star of true light from Himself, the true knowledge of Himself, that star of which He speaks when He says, "I am the root and the offspring of David, and the bright and morning star." When He shines into the soul, to him that conquers selfishness and evil, He is, first of all, a "morning star," an inward heavenly light that tells him of a new day, which assures him the night is ended and his morning is beginning. But that same star will enlarge, will become grander as he presses on, until it will become from a star at length, the great Sun of righteousness, that with healing in its wings will shed its whole blessings upon him.

When religion is corrupted, when the church is fallen, then men make use of the knowledge they have of heavenly things, not for heavenly purposes, but for earthly ones, the stars fall from heaven. They care nothing about heaven, they make pelf and power the great objects of their concern; they talk about Scripture, they preach like saints: they make use of religion as if they were the most earnest men in the world; but it is self that is at the bottom, it is some earthly advantage; they talk of God, but mean themselves; they talk of religion, but mean getting a good living by it; they bring the stars down from heaven, and mix them up with their own life, their own low and selfish persuasions and feelings. This is when the stars fall from heaven. It has nothing to do with the wreck of the outward universe, it is the wreck of their inward universe. The stars fall from heaven.

But man's necessity is God's opportunity. When men have come to the end, then is the time for God to begin. The darkest hour of the night is that just before the morning. And hence, directly after the passage has stated that all the great lights are darkened, come the words of restoration: "Then shall appear the sign of the Son of man in Heaven"—the sign of the Son of man—the banner of the Son of man. For this is what the "sign" means—the banner, the flag, as it were, the ensign—the true symbol of the Son of man. The ensign of an army is the banner by which it is known where the general is, where the headquarters of the army are, for there the banner of the chieftain waves. Thus it is known where the ruler is. The sign of the Son of man is the true doctrine of Jesus Christ. His banner is the doctrine which declares who He is, what He is, and what He requires. "Then shall the sign of the Son of man appear in heaven." That is to say, Thus will the Lord Jesus make Himself known afresh in His true and perfect character; so that men may know that God is Jesus Christ, the manifest Deity, and that they must be like-minded with Jesus Christ, or they are no Christians.

This true doctrine, which would be unveiled when a new dispensation, or a new heaven and earth, were to be formed, is in this blessed book called "the sign of the Son of man." It is promised in other parts of the sacred Scriptures. Jesus said, "The time cometh when I will show you plainly of the Father." Plainly. But except in the New Church, which has been revealed in these latter days, men know no more of the Father than the Jews did. In the New Jerusalem it is seen that Jesus Christ Himself is what Isaiah taught He was, when He said, "For unto us a child is born, unto us a son is given; and the government shall be upon his shoulder, and his name shall be called Wonderful, Counseller, The mighty God, the Everlasting Father, The Prince of peace." The doctrine that teaches this, teaches "plainly of the Father." Jesus Christ has the Father in Him, like a man has the soul in him. "The Father who is in me, He doeth the works."

In this way we perceive how plainly the Father is revealed to us in the Divine Saviour, and that no man can come to the Father but through Him and by Him. He that seeth Him seeth the Father: and this is the plain teaching of the Father, "the sign of the Son of man in heaven." When persons separated from Jesus Christ the idea of the Godhead, so that they worshipped two other distinct persons or Gods, whom they called the First Person, and the Third Person, some imagined this God was of such a character, that He had only made a few to be saved; others, that He was of such a character, that it was excessively difficult to please Him; and although they would readily go to Jesus Christ for mercy and salvation, they dreaded the others, particularly the first. They must be continually mortifying themselves, not only in wrong things, but in right things; making themselves miserable all their lives long, not enjoying the beauties of their Father's world, or the mercies of their Father. This is not the plain teaching of the Father. Hence, creeds which were made general in the middle ages say, "The Father is incomprehensible, the Son is incomprehensible, and the Holy Ghost is incomprehensible." That is not the plain doctrine of the Father, nor of the Son. That which is "incomprehensible" cannot be plain; and hence, those who adhere to this creed attempt to stop investigation by saying it is a great mystery. "You must not think about it; it is a mystery." Well, so it is, but that is not the plain teaching of the Father. These persons put their own sign up, that they are not what Jesus Christ declared would be, for He says that the time would come when He would teach us plainly of the Father. These persons say their teaching is incomprehensible. You are, then, only a provisional church; you are confessedly not what Jesus meant, when He said, "The time cometh when He would show men plainly of the Father."

In other parts of the sacred Scriptures it is said, the "knowledge of the Lord should cover the earth as the waters cover the sea."—Isa. xi. 6. This was to be another sign of the second coming of the Saviour. "The knowledge of the Lord should cover the earth." This prophecy has to be fulfilled undoubtedly. How few yet know the Lord truly! Those called Christians are not a fourth of the human race. Of these, is one in a hundred really so? Of these, how many have a CLEAR KNOWLEDGE of the Lord? The prophecy has not been fulfilled, and how can it ever be fulfilled with the Church's present mysterious doctrines? Ponder this well. The knowledge of that which cannot be known never can cover the earth. The ordinary churches confess they have not a knowledge of God. They sometimes try to prove it cannot be had. We believe the Scriptures, and are convinced there is a knowledge of God that can be comprehended. When this is done—when men can have such a knowledge of God as they can see to be first scriptural, then rational, and then in harmony with all that science discovers, then each man, and every man, aye, and every woman, and every intelligent child too, can give to the heathen, to Mahommedan, to Jews, to all classes of men, the knowledge of the Lord, that may, and will, cover the earth as the waters cover the sea. But this will, not come till men have been taught that He who said, "Ye call me Master and Lord, and ye say well, for so I am," is the real Lord Jehovah of the Old Testament as well as Jesus of the New; the only God of the universe, by whom all things were made, without whom has not anything been made that has been made.—John i. 3.

The next grand feature which is connected with the revelation of the Son of man in this and other parts of the sacred Scriptures is, that there should be such a state of innocence by walking in the Lord's path, as that, in the beautiful language of the eleventh chapter of Isaiah, none "shall hurt nor destroy in all my holy mountain." That passage has not yet been fulfilled. Those who read over the sad pages of the dark history of what has been called the church, for hundreds of years gone by, will find it has been very far from none hurting nor destroying in all God's holy mountain. It has been one man calling himself a Christian, yet injuring another as much as he well could. The men of one system persecuting another as much as they well could. Nay, not only Christian nations struggling and fighting amongst themselves, but struggling and fighting against one another. We have only just come out of a tremendous effort of our own in that style,* very far from none hurting nor destroying in God's holy mountain; very far from what the Scriptures teach, that the time shall come when men "shall beat their swords into ploughshares, and their spears into pruning-hooks; nation shall not lift up sword against nation, neither shall they learn war any more." Oh no, brethren, with the common Christianity, which ignores the fact that God is Divine love and wisdom, true peace can never be. An angry God makes angry Christians, a sectarian God makes sectarian Christians. There must be new principles, surrounded with such a glory of heavenly light as is called in our text "power and great glory." Power—the power of practical religion; the power of a religion, clear and loving, that is no contradiction in itself—that does not say it is, and it is not; that to repent and be good is the way to be saved, and yet that the vilest murderers, whose lives have been a chain of crimes, can be saved by believing at the last. The power of religion that has no back doors to heaven, that says the soul must really be trained for heaven by actually living a godly life, is real life, is real power. If you put it off until you hope to make

* The Russian War.

it up by a little faith at last, you may depend upon it you are not taking Christ's method. Christ says, "Not every one that saith unto me Lord, Lord, shall enter into the kingdom of heaven; but he that DOETH THE WILL of my Father who is in heaven." People generally, and especially religious teachers, have been too fond of talking about the dying part of religion, and too little intent, either in precept or in practice, to the living part of religion. No religion can really operate a change in human souls, in nations, and in the world, but a religion that teaches men how to live; and which tells them if they live aright their death is sure to come aright. It must be a religion that begins with childhood, a religion that says, "Suffer little children to come unto me." To COME UNTO ME! This is one of the most cheering signs of the new age.

We have begun in these latter days to be very anxious and earnest about little children. Sunday schools have arisen within the last hundred years, and are one of the grandest fruits of the second outpouring of Divine love. Sunday schools are indeed a move in the right direction. They take little children and train them to live, but unhappily they too often have not had full, free, and fair effect. The religion given in too many Sunday schools has been imparted to the scholars in such an unpleasant style, and is itself so sectarian and comfortless, that the schools become distasteful. The children are crammed with catechisms and made miserable by gloomy tales of hell, instead of gently giving them here a little and there a little of the beautiful, the true, and the good, in heaven and earth. The little souls are often frightened with the description of a terrible God, instead of being attracted by a God of kindness and love—one who takes them to His arms and blesses them. Fear has been the great exciting stimulant by which men have been called to God in the old religion. The new religion has for its grand principle Love—Christ as a God of love—religion as a religion of love. Heaven is the land of love; the Bible is the narration of love, when it is truly understood. And this grand principle operating with children, so as to lead them to love religion—not to be frightened into it, and terrified with everything about it; to love it as the way to happiness; to enable them to live in religion when they are living on earth, as the true way of happiness; to overcome in themselves what opposes religion, as the only mode of cleansing out the sources of misery; to exhort and teach children to remove from themselves that self-love which has been the gall of bitterness in past ages, and will be so to them if they do not begin to fight against it, and obey, the Divine Saviour and His laws,—this is the essential lesson. This is the spirit of the new dispensation. This is the new proclamation; the banner of the Son of man. And when this spirit, combined with reason, seen to be in harmony with religion and science—seen, I say, to be in harmony with both, is accepted, it will present us with the principles which, when spread, will really cause none to hurt, none to destroy, in all God's holy mountain.

The same period of the latter days is represented in the Scriptures to be a period of light—a period of intelligence. And true religion is, and must be really so. It is only a mistaken religion that has an inward fear of its principles, that keeps continually saying to men, "Now don't you reason about them, you will get into infidelity if you don't mind; you must not be too eager about science, science reveals some very strange things; science teaches one thing and religion another." The religion which opposes as long as it can the teachings of science, and when it cannot oppose further, modifies as little as it can, is a religion you should suspect. It is a mistaken theology. True theology is in all respects harmonious with itself, it harmonises with its God, harmonises with science, and harmonises with true reason: it comes to man "with power and great glory." "The tribes of the earth," it is said, "mourn." Those that have believed previously in other views and in other principles, mourn at first; they don't like it, change is sad for them. To part with old notions, prejudices, and beliefs, is always something difficult. We have all mourned when it has been found that false principles have been prevalent with us, and we have to change our views and habits; but "Blessed are they that mourn, for they shall be comforted." Let persons always remember, however, that although they may view the new light and the new principles as taking away things that have been dearly cherished, if they find these things to be unsound, let them bear in mind that he who passes from error to truth gains a reward to overpay him for any mourning, any difficulty, any degree of pain or agitation—he cannot but gain in this glorious conflict. He who loses wins. He who finds he has been mistaken before, but now embraces a higher and nobler view, he is the gainer. When two are considering a subject, the person who has had the right side, when the argument is finished, is where he was; but the person who has had the wrong side loses the argument, but he gains the truth, which is a thousand times better.

And as the influence of these sacred principles from the Most High, meant by the new city, the heavenly Jerusalem coming down from God, spread, as these principles extend, not by man's discovery, but by God's revelation, the Saviour is coming, will come. His spreading light, His spreading love are leading men to become truly brothers, more and more. It is breaking out sometimes in one direction, sometimes in another, and it is advancing gradually, as God does everything, but really with rapid and giant strides. He never flashes from night to day all at once. It is in the moral world as it is in the material. The sun rises gradually —tips first the top of the eastern hills—gradually extends his beams down their sloping sides, over the plains, and over the fields, until, at length, his silent majesty diffuses over the face of nature its glorious light, and the whole horizon is illuminated. Just so it is in the moral and spiritual worlds. Truth always begins with the few. There were only the eleven disciples that met after Jesus was crucified; only eleven of them that met together. They were shut up in a house for fear of the Jews; but from these went forth the new light, which was taken up by another band at the time of Pentecost. This gradually spread itself through the first century—onwards it went, until the banner of the Saviour, despised as it had been, was bowed down to by the chiefs of the earth, and the cross that had been a disgrace became a glory. And so it is always. God begins with a few. He touches some noble holy souls with the rising light of a new day. It is like the glittering summit of the highest mountain that gets its first glories, and reflects its brilliancy to another and another; God's truths become gradually unfolded, and first one and then another receives them, and still fresh souls widen the circle, until at length that which was known at first only to a few becomes spread throughout the world. And so will it be—it is coming, not by outward observation, but by inward diffusion. There are men with principles of this class being formed amongst all the denominations. Those that love God are gradually receiving views more worthy of God; and this diffusion of Divine truth, partly through a few men, but really from the great Lord of lords will leaven the whole world. It has commenced its glorious career; it will never cease. "I beheld One that sat upon the throne," wrote the Apostle John, who said, "I am Alpha and Omega, the beginning and the end;" who said also, "Whosoever will, let him take of the water of life freely;" and He said, "Behold, I make all things new." He has again made His spiritual coming; again new things have been poured out amongst mankind; again the glorious light has been spreading, and will spread, until the realization to the finest minds of the scriptural prophecies—the realization of men's hopes and feelings and anticipations will be altogether expanded into the universal brotherhood of good and holy men, that do justly, love mercy, and walk humbly with their God; under the fatherhood of the Lord Jesus Christ, "in whom dwells all the fulness of the Godhead bodily." He will be seen reigning over their souls, and thus reigning over their bodies, until that glorious period is consummated and realised which the prophets have foretold, and all the great souls of poetry have sung, which every good man anticipates, desires, and strives for ; the crown of all toil, the perfection of all ages, the reward of all suffering ; earth's imitation of heaven, the true establishment of the unfailing nursery for angels.

> "Then let us pray, that come it may,
> As come it will for a' that,
> When sense and worth, o'er a' the earth,
> Shall bear the gree, and a' that:
> For a' that, and a' that,
> It's coming yet, for a' that,
> When man to man, the world o'er,
> Shall brothers be, and a' that."

THE DISCUSSION.

The Rev. Mr. ———: I am a clergyman of the Church of England, and while agreeing with much that I have heard, yet I must object to your reference to the Athanasian Creed. You seem to think that all persons who use the word "incomprehensible" in the creed, do so in a sense meaning not capable of being understood, and that persons attached to that creed show their absurdity in so saying. I am not used to public speaking; but I take it to mean, according to the original, "infinite," not able to be grasped. The Father infinite, the Son infinite, and the Holy Ghost infinite—I take that to be the meaning of incomprehensible, and the English word admits of that interpretation.

Dr. BAYLEY: I am perfectly aware that there are many, and I hope the number will still increase, who interpret the word "incomprehensible" in the sense that you have given it, and which appears to me to be quite unobjectionable. There are a very large number, however, who do not at all use it in that sense; and I should venture almost to say that it must be within your own experience that such is the case. Probably you have had to correct people who have drawn the idea from that word "incomprehensible," that God cannot be comprehended at all. It is so very common a thing, or else I have had an unusual lot in meeting chiefly with those who hold that creed, and who represent God as incomprehensible, in the sense of not being capable of being understood in any way. I have wished very much oftener to have met with your version than I have.

CLERGYMAN: I think you did not think of the true meaning of it when you referred to it, or if you did, you did not clearly prove what you intended, and which I think you would desire to impress.

Dr. BAYLEY: I am exceedingly obliged to you for drawing attention to the circumstance. Of course, in our observations we are frequently obliged to omit a great many exceptional feelings and statements which, at other times, perhaps, are brought strikingly forward, and it is a happy thing when, on such an occasion, a friend will take the opportunity which you have taken, of throwing some light upon a subject that has been overlooked. At the same time I am fully satisfied that the idea you have given is not the general idea in the Church of England—that it is an exceptional view ("No, no")—and that the general notion is, that the doctrine of the Godhead is a great mystery that cannot be understood. (A voice: "So it is.") A friend says, so it is; and that is the common idea, and to this common idea I have addressed myself. There are a few who are like our friend, and who are willing to interpret the Athanasian Creed in a different style, and I hope our friend's body will increase.

CLERGYMAN: I did not mean to say that that was the general acceptation of the term, but that it was the right way of interpretation. I know the other view is a popular delusion, and great numbers think God cannot be comprehended; but I hardly think that justifies your attack on the Athanasian Creed.

Dr. BAYLEY: Our friend admits that what I have described is a popular delusion, and this is chiefly grounded on the Athanasian Creed, which entirely justifies my referring to it. I did not refer to it as an attack on the Athanasian Creed, but as the impression that people largely have in relation to God. I spoke to the popular mind, and spoke of a popular delusion. If I had been attacking the Athanasian Creed, I can assure our friend it would hardly have been in so tender a style. I have not the slightest respect for it. I believe it to be a tissue of contradictions from first to last. ("No, no.") It says the thing of which it speaks is a great mystery, and then it proceeds to explain it, and, in this pretended explanation, contradicts itself in sentence after sentence. After giving what the unknown author intends for an explanation, but which is a series of contradictions, he then declares three times over that no one can be saved unless he accepts undoubtedly his very questionable explanation of this great mystery. For such a creed I have not the slightest respect. (Cheers and hisses.) The applause or the hisses will have nothing to do with the argument—we should endeavour to preserve ourselves, if possible, for argument—noise never proves anything. As soon as there is manly feeling enough in the leaders of the Church of England to dare to be faithful to the truth, and to alter their creed and catechisms, they will not let our great dignitaries get up in the House of Lords and confess that these things must not be altered because destruction will follow. When the people become thoughtful enough to say, "We will have the truth, and nothing but good will follow," I believe one of the first things will be the blotting out of the Athanasian Creed. (Cheers.) Archbishop Tillotson, the once great leader of the Bishops of England, wished they were well rid of it. Many, both clergy and people, wish still they were rid of it. Our friend, as a clergyman, will know, that although the creed is said to be that of St. Athanasius, there is a great doubt as to whether he wrote it, or, rather, it is certain he did not write it. It is thought by many that Vigilius, an African Bishop, composed it. It is a creed that professes to explain what it cannot explain, and then damns all that do not receive it. (Hear, hear.) A friend said lately that a clergyman had suggested to him that if it are always recited in Latin it would not be felt to be so severe as when read in English. Perhaps that would be best, as the first step towards getting rid of it. If it were always read in Latin, so that no one understood it, there would not be much harm. (A laugh, and cheers.)

ANOTHER GENTLEMAN: You, sir, did not come to Brighton, I am sure, with these truths in your mind without being perfectly certain that you would come against the grain of most men's ordinary belief. You did not come here without being pretty well prepared to be called names—to be told you were heretic. But, sir, I remember in ancient history a story told of a practical shrewd man, whom I have no doubt his fellow-tradesmen called a most sagacious man—a man named Demetrius—who, when Christianity came, felt that his craft was in danger, and cried out "Great is Diana of the Ephesians." Those whose craft is in danger will cry out, but nevertheless truth must prevail. The world is really on the move once more. Men's souls are being stirred towards a better way; and, sir, until the clergy learn to understand what feeling is lying underneath the conviction and the expressed belief of the intelligent laity of the Church of England, I say, sir, her influence will be diminished, is diminishing, and ought to diminish. The truths you have told me, and that you have announced in your visits here this time, are identical with what for twelve years I have obscurely been working out on my part with an agony of brain, which perhaps you can scarcely give credit for in these days of easy popular religion and platform oratory. I say it is true that our teachers, not merely the Church of England, but our popular teachers, have always taught in a mere forensic tone a scheme more fitted for a *nisi prius* lawyer. I say, sir, that these are the teachers that make our infidels. We can believe in the infinite Love that created us and sustained us, and which, we are told, has redeemed us—we can believe such doctrines as these—but some men will tell us that these things are "cunningly devised fables," and that we want ancient creed-made truth.

No, sir, we want clear distinct declarations flowing from that simple truth, the infinite love of God. I dare not enter into the questions that you have brought before us; I cannot say that I yield them my entire assent, although I have no antagonistic doctrine which I can bring against them. For any man to stand up and say he has got the whole truth, is as absurd as if he were to go to the sea-side and fill a tiny vessel with water, and say he had got the whole waters of the ocean. Truth is a glorious system of many sides; and he will do the Church an infinite service who will distinguish from outward creed and ceremonies the spiritual good that lies underneath. When that is done we shall have men really practical, living Christians; and, sir, I feel that I am not merely thanking you in my own name, when I propose a vote of thanks, but in the names of most here, when I thank you for the truth preached here at Brighton. (Loud cheers.) I hope these germs of holy thought will be to many of us germs of holy obedience. I trust, sir, that your present visit will not be the last. (Hear, hear.) I never saw you before I saw you stand at that table, and now I feel that what you have said is real, spiritual, rational truth, and food for the thirsty soul; and as such I bid you "God speed" in your work. (Loud cheers.)

Dr. BAYLEY: Suffer me, my beloved friend, to thank you also.

The clergyman here intimated he joined in the vote of thanks, though he dissented from some few of the sentiments.

Dr. BAYLEY: You have my kindest thanks for your remarks, and for the manner in which you made them. I cannot but be gratified at the little incidents that have arisen out of them. I assure you it is not any conventional thing when an invitation is given by me to the audience to make remarks—to offer difficulties. I feel there is living beauty in Divine truths that will give to us comfort in time and happiness in death, if we understand and love them. In connection with the principles that I have been endeavouring to give to my fellow-men, exist clearness, harmony, and peace. I have had many of the same difficulties to master, the same objections to review and to go through that others may be feeling at the very time that they are invited to hear. When we view the subjects in the way we have been presenting them, we shall get light where there was darkness, confidence where there was hesitation, and harmony with science and reason where there seemed to be contradiction and difficulty. It is to help many to understand and explain these things that I have ventured to come to Brighton. I am exceedingly grateful for the kind and brotherly attention that has been paid to me both by the clergy and others who have brought their particular views under our notice; I have endeavoured to receive them, in a brotherly way,—and now I trust we shall part with a determination to "search the Scriptures," as the fountains of truth, to see whether these things be so. Let us dare to "prove all things, and hold fast that which is good," and determinately to have our hearts set upon working out our salvation, both in truth and in goodness, with fear and trembling, but certainly with the conviction that God will never, never deny His light to a seeking, earnest, loving spirit. Let us make the determination that we will take up the maxim of the beautiful spirit of Cowper—

> "And truth alone, where'er my life be cast,
> In scenes of plenty or the pining waste,
> Shall be my chosen theme, my glory to the last."

Allow me to wish you, then, an affectionate "Good night," and to express a most earnest desire for your success in your spiritual and in your earthly endeavours. Allow me to say "God speed" in your spirit's work, under the protection of Him who is Love itself and Truth itself. (Loud cheers.)

Mr. MOTT, surgeon, in the chair: I humbly request your attention for a few moments this evening—this being the last lecture the Rev. Doctor will give in the present course. They have been given gratis—no expense whatever being incurred by any person in Brighton; everything has been done gratuitously.* We have heard six most eloquent, striking, interesting lectures upon the most important points that involve the welfare of man's life, both here and for eternity, and I think you will agree with me that we ought all to join once more in giving a vote of thanks to the Rev. Doctor for his kindly coming here and delivering to us these lectures. (Loud cheers.)

Rev. J. Ross: I think the eloquent lecturer has acquitted himself as a workman that needeth not be ashamed (Hear, hear); and if there are any in this assembly who dissent—and I believe some will think differently from him—yet we must all agree that he has shown a singular Christian-mindedness in his mode of stating truth, and great ability and clearness in the proclamation of his own views. (Applause.) I am afraid, sirs, that my testimony will not be of much service to Dr. Bayley, who, like myself, has been considered to be an heretic—I, sir, have suffered for the proclamation of many of those truths which Dr. Bayley, with more eloquence than myself, has delivered in the course of these six lectures. (Hear, hear.) I am not ashamed to give my testimony; and in order to gather up into a focus the chief points or principles in which I coincide with Dr. Bayley, I will just distinctly state them. First. He has done great service in this town in proclaiming that "God is one" (hear, and cheers)—that there is a baptism that teaches us that we are baptised not into three names, but One infinitely Divine name, the name of that Saviour who is Father, Son, and Holy Spirit; whereas, the common Christianity teaches that there is a severance of persons in the Divinity. Dr. Bayley has done great service to God's truth in teaching us, secondly, That the atonement is a thing not wrought to change God's mind, but that it was a great process in which God's mind was revealed to the world; the Scriptures never say that Christ reconciled God to man, but, on the contrary, that "God was in Christ, reconciling the world to Himself." Thirdly: Dr. Bayley has done great service

* Subsequently, friends in Brighton insisted upon paying the

in teaching, in re-stating, the apostolic doctrine of the resurrection from the dead, and the rising up of the spiritual man from the mortal clay. When the work has been done with the mortal body, we then come forth in what is called the immortal, the principle within, which rises up to the Eternal for ever. But, last of all, Dr. Bayley deserves our cordial thanks for proclaiming that the first, midmost, and last feature in religion is charity. God is love; Christ is the love of God seen in the flesh. One word, sir: I feel that I must disburden my conscience: I am not going to controvert any statement of yours; I feel that the last place in the world for the discussion of truth is a popular assembly, yet I preach as I believe, and that is, that God's charity will never rest satisfied while a man remains in the hells of selfishness. No man, however, can be saved by simply saying that he believes. He must subdue sin, and work out his salvation; God never changes. He always does His utmost to enable man to follow Him; and if man does so, he will find that God is all in all. And now, my dear friend, I cordially thank you, and I am sure all this audience does, for your kindness in coming to Brighton, and for the ability you have shown in delivering these lectures, and I beg to second the motion. (Cheers.)

The resolution was then put and carried with but one dissentient hand being held up.

It was then resolved to request that Dr. Bayley should revisit Brighton at his earliest convenience, which also was carried with the solitary hand only being held up for the negative.

Dr. BAYLEY: I beg, my dear friends, to thank you all for your courtesy and kind feeling. I assure you that this meeting has been a sufficient inducement to dispose me to visit Brighton again early. I thank our dissenting friend, too, for bravely putting himself in opposition to the whole meeting when he thought he was right. He stands up for what he believes to be the truth, and he should be held worthy of all respect as a brave and worthy man. (Loud cheers.)

www.ingramcontent.com/pod-product-compliance
Lightning Source LLC
Chambersburg PA
CBHW020821230426
43666CB00007B/1053